SOME DAYS
I THINK I'LL LIVE

CHRISTINE M. STANFIELD

Some days I think I'll live...

THOMAS NELSON PUBLISHERS
Nashville

Published in Nashville, Tennessee, by Thomas Nelson, Inc., and distributed in Canada by Lawson Falle, Ltd., Cambridge, Ontario.

Printed in the United States of America.

Library of Congress Cataloging-in-Publication Data

Stanfield, Christine M.
    Some days I think I'll live / Christine M. Stanfield.
    Includes bibliographical references.
    ISBN 0-8407-7452-4
    1. Divorce—United States—Case studies. 2. Divorced women—
    United States—Psychology—Case studies. 3. Divorce—Religious
    aspects—Christianity. I. Title.
    HQ834.S72   1991
    306.89—dc20   90–42776
                                                              CIP

Printed in the United States of America

1 2 3 4 5 6 7 — 95 94 93 92 91 90

This book is dedicated
to all the people in my life
who have encouraged me
and stood by me through the hard times

A very special thanks to God

CONTENTS

CHAPTER ONE

Surgery

I've been recovering from domestic surgery—a radical husbandectomy and a partial childectomy—more commonly known as divorce with shared custody of the child.

God said there would be tribulation: "In the world you will have tribulation" (John 16:33a). He was right.

So, why was I surprised when I found myself in the midst of this particular big time tribulation? Because God hates divorce. So do I. But, that didn't change the facts—my husband of fourteen years chose to leave.

My flesh would love to get into some heavy duty name-calling right now, but my spirit knows better. Besides, in order to be fair, I'd have to call myself names too. In most cases, it takes two to make it, two to break it. In our case, it broke.

For some time, after my husband moved out, I

felt completely lost in my emotions. But, eventually, I did ask myself the logical question: What should I do now? Seek legal counsel, of course.

That sounded like a plan, until I discovered how expensive attorney's fees are. "No problem," I thought. "I'll do it myself."

Courthouse Games

I started at the county courthouse, where I found myself standing in a line to pick up the necessary papers. While waiting, I read the sign above the window. "It is unlawful for any court employee to give legal advice." (I wonder whose idea that was?)

When it was my turn, I asked, "Could you please give me the necessary papers for a divorce?"

**It is unlawful for any court
employee to give legal advice.**

The lady inside the window looked at me sympathetically. "I can't tell you what kind of papers you need," she said.

Okay, I get it, this is a game. "Do I have to guess?" I asked.

She said nothing but nodded her head up and down. Ah-ha, it must be charades!

This lady must have had a soft spot in her heart, because she surreptitiously laid some papers out on the counter. We both looked around to be sure no one was watching. I picked three forms.

"You might as well take two more, because they are five for twenty-five cents," she offered.

All right! Now, those are the kind of prices I like. I took two more. By their titles, I was confident they could get the job done. When I inquired as to where I could get some assistance in filling out the forms, the nice lady pointed to another window.

As I stood in line number two, I read the forms, just in case I could figure them out myself. No chance. After fifteen minutes, it was my turn at the head of the line. Above that window, there were two signs—one said "OSC DIVORCE." I thought, "Now we're cooking!" The other sign said "It is unlawful for any court employee to give legal advice." I was starting to get a little frustrated.

The lady behind this window stuck to the rule book. She stated firmly, "I can't answer any questions."

Defending my position, I said, "But I was told that you could help me with these forms."

13

She must have been having a bad morning. "Whoever told you that was wrong. Next!"

A man in line behind me suggested I try the Civil Window. He looked official with his nice suit and big briefcase, so I took his advice. As I moved to the new line, I hoped that whoever was behind this window would indeed be civil.

Of course, window number three had a sign above it. To break the monotony, however, this sign had a slight variation on the theme. "We cannot give any legal advice including how to fill out forms."

I made another attempt to decipher the forms on my own. The only thing I could figure out was that I needed one more form.

I went back to window number one where I'd had the only success of the day. I explained that one of my forms seemed to indicate that I needed a corresponding form to go along with it. The nice lady nodded again. She brought over a form and asked me if there was any form I had that I would like to trade for this new one. "Why not? Now we're playing cards," I thought. "I'll give you one 'writ of execution' for one 'contempt,'" I said.

We made the trade. The game was over. She suggested that I go to the law library. I said to myself, "Why not law school?"

14

"My brethren, count it all joy when you fall into various trials, knowing that the testing of your faith produces patience" (James 1:2–3).

Court Dates

Needless to say, I hired an attorney shortly after my do-it-yourself experience.

Divorce attorneys—they're fun. Enough said. My guess is you've already experienced first-hand or heard enough lawyer stories, so I'll spare you a possible rise in your blood pressure.

Divorce attorneys—they're fun.

Divorce trials—they're interesting, in a maso-chistic sort of way. "The system" treats you as if you weren't already facing enough pain, humiliation, and confusion.

Divorce trials—they're interesting, in a masochistic sort of way.

Attorneys introduce you to what laymen call "no-fault divorce"—let's hear it for complete denial! I'm assuming the theory behind it is "why point fingers?" We all know that the divorce fairy comes along and sprinkles separation dust on a couple, and *voila!* Off to an easy trial they go.

In order to keep everything appropriately impersonal, various generic titles and terms are used: petitioner, respondent, minor child, adult, each party (I don't feel like a party), noncustodial parent, spousal support, child support, custody, alternating visitations (sounds like a day in the park—it isn't), and dissolution.

I was terribly frightened my first day at court; surprised, as well. My husband's attorney and my attorney went into the courtroom, had some papers stamped, and then retired to a table in the cafeteria—an appropriate enough spot to work out some of the details of their clients' lives.

We clients didn't even participate. We just sat at opposite ends of the room and waited for the attorneys to wave us over when they were ready to tell us what they had decided.

"My soul, wait silently for God alone, for my expectation is from Him. He only is my

rock and my salvation; He is my defense; I shall not be moved" (Ps. 62:5–6).

The next event was called a preliminary trial. I thought we'd be going before a judge this time, but that wasn't the case. There was no judge in the courtroom. I found out later that he was in his chamber.

My soon-to-be-ex-mate went into a side room with his attorney, where they whispered. When they were done, my attorney and his attorney went into the room and whispered. Then, my attorney and I went into the same room and whispered. Everyone whispered, except the lady who stamped papers.

Eventually, both attorneys went into the judge's chamber to discuss in secret the dividing of our lives. Great idea! I never saw the man who was making decisions that would affect years of my life.

The final trial date found us in a scheduling room at 7:30 A.M. A note on the door of our assigned room indicated that the judge was too busy with a previous trial to take us.

On our rescheduled day the judge asked us to come back in the afternoon. When we returned, the court was still in session. More waiting, with attorney fee-meters running the whole time, of course. My stress level was maxed out.

As you might imagine, God heard from me almost constantly during these proceedings.

> *"Be anxious for nothing, but in everything by prayer and supplication, with thanksgiving, let your requests be made known to God; and the peace of God, which surpasses all understanding, will guard your hearts and minds through Christ Jesus" (Phil. 4:6–7).*

Philippians 4:6–7 became particularly significant to me at this time. I personalized it, and recited it again and again. I did, however, have little arguments with myself as I tried to put into practice the principles of the verse.

"Chris, be anxious for nothing," I'd tell myself. "Are you sure *nothing* includes divorce and all that goes along with it?" I'd want to know. It must. Nothing means "no thing." Making my prayer requests to God was fairly easy. But thanking Him for this ordeal was extremely difficult. The promise that the peace of God would guard my heart and mind through Jesus Christ reminded me that Jesus suffered for me far beyond anything I could ever imagine. The fact that He loved me that much made me feel secure and that He would be there for me no matter what. And that helped me to experience moments, at least, of peace that definitely did surpass my understanding.

". . . be anxious for nothing," I'd tell myself.

The Final Events

As I fought the early morning rush hour traffic on the way to the final day in court, I also fought those feelings of anxiety I'd been trying so hard to overcome. As I walked from the parking lot to the courthouse, I felt like a five year old going to my first day of school. I had little idea of what to expect, and I would have felt a lot more secure if I'd had someone to come along with me and hold my hand.

I didn't have anyone to come along with me on that first day of school, and I didn't have anyone this day either. But, I did have prayer, and I tried to think about something positive. Paul, my eleven-year-old son, came to mind. Although the dividing of things was important, none of that mattered nearly as much as the arrangements regarding him. And fortunately, that was one issue we had been able to settle out of court.

I wanted Paul to live with me full-time, and his father wanted him full-time. Obviously, we could not incorporate both plans, so we made an equitable arrangement. Paul would live with me for half of the year and then with his dad for the other half of the year. The noncustodial parent would see Paul on Wednesday evenings and every other weekend.

My thoughts turned back to the task at hand, as I opened the courthouse door. I found the courtroom with a judge on the stand, a court recorder, and a bailiff, to be very intimidating, especially since my only previous experiences have been vicarious ones, through TV and the movies. This wasn't pretend. It was real life—my life—drama. I had been concerned that I might cry the whole time; but, as it turned out, I was too scared to cry at all.

Many of the specifics of the ordeal aren't clear to me now. And that's okay with me—it isn't something I want to treasure in my memory bank. But a few impressions remain with me anyway.

The term *trial* seemed very appropriate for the situation. Sitting on the stand was extremely uncomfortable. The cold, calculating manner in which I was interrogated by the other attorney made me feel like I was a criminal. Almost every answer led to another question. The judge didn't make it any easier. Instead of listening attentively, he whispered to his assistant a couple of times while I was talking. And I got the distinct impression that he wasn't even slightly interested in what was going on.

I felt numb as I sat at the attorney's table waiting for the judge to wrap it up. I did have one comforting thought—Paul had not been required to go through such an experience.

I think the proceedings lasted two hours. Maybe not. One thing is certain, they were too long. I thanked God it was over. At least these times of having personal matters dissected and rearranged by people who didn't really care what happened to me were concluded.

I felt relieved and drained as I drove home. The radical changes in my life were now legal, confirmed by the judge's stamp. Almost everything would be different—except God. He and His love for me remained the same.

> *"And we know that all things work together for good to those who love God, to those who are the called according to His purpose"* *(Rom. 8:28).*

CHAPTER TWO

Post Op: Give Me
a Tourniquet

Surgery left me with plenty of pain.

"So, Doc, I don't feel very good. Did you and your team of surgeons have to do anything else when I was opened up?" I asked.

"Actually, we did. You were aware of the husband and child removal part. But we were also forced to remove half—well, maybe a little more—of everything you owned. We also lowered your self-confidence, but that can be brought back up with proper care. Your role in society has been altered, too. Instead of being a wife and mother, you're now a divorced woman, the head of a single-parent home. The good news is you still have your heart. It's a little tattered, but it should heal in a year or two," he said reassuringly.

"It sounds like I'll be in recovery for awhile. So when will I be able to go home?" I inquired.

"Right now. The nurse will be here in a minute with your discharge papers and a wheel-chair."

"What? How can that be? I'm still bleeding. I'm too weak!"

"Sorry. We need your bed. You know how popular this operation is these days. We have a long waiting list."

"But I don't have anyone to take care of me."

"This will be good practice for you. You may be taking care of yourself for quite some time. Besides, you can always get into a therapy program when you can afford it. Good luck," he said cheerfully.

"How did my son, Paul, fare through all of this?"

"He'll be in recovery for some time, too. He will also have scars—that's to be expected. But he'll be fine."

"Thanks," I mumbled, devoid of enthusiasm.

"But those who wait on the LORD shall renew their strength; they shall mount up with wings like eagles, they shall run and not be weary, they shall walk and not faint" (Isa. 40:31).

It amazed me how many things suddenly seemed trivial when something so very important—my family—was shaken, changed, and either partially or totally taken away.

As a Christian, how long am I allowed to grieve?

This makes me wonder: As a Christian, how long am I allowed to grieve? How long am I allowed to hurt? I don't just have to grin and bear it, but what do I do instead? A rule book would sure be helpful, with a section on the appropriate lengths for pity parties. Mate leaves: one year, six months, or two days—depending on how fond you were of your mate. Child leaves: a lifetime, two months, or one week—depending on the age and mischievousness of the child, perhaps. The dog leaves with your child (part of any good custody settlement): two days, half a day, or five minutes—depending on how much it barks, chews furniture, "oh-no's" on the carpet.

On second thought, I doubt that such a book would work. It would be too difficult to create one that would apply to everyone's personal experience. Oh, well. It was just a thought. I'm always on the lookout for anything that might make "getting it right" a little easier.

"Trust in the Lord with all your heart, and lean not on your own understanding; in

27

*all your ways acknowledge Him, and He
shall direct your paths" (Prov. 3:5–6).*

My first year of separation was the worst. I experienced tons of pain and loneliness and grief,
fear, guilt, resentment, anger . . . My main
source of strength was God. With His grace and
love, as well as the support of some relatives and
friends, I kept my head above water.

While treading those murky, troubled waters,
I had some bad ideas. For example, I wasn't
always wise in how I shared my story. Maybe I
thought I didn't have enough people to talk to, or
maybe I just had too many emotions welling up
within me, ready to spill out of my mouth without first going through "verbal-tactfulness qual-
ity control." Whatever the reason, I occasionally
found myself talking too openly with people I
didn't know well.

It seemed I'd most often run into these folks
in the supermarket. They would greet me with
"Hi, Chris, how are you doing?" I'd answer, "Oh,
not so good. My husband left me. We had been
married for fourteen years, you know." My blunt
responses basically shocked them, I think. Most
people just want you to say "fine," even if you are
dying inside. They don't want you to bleed all
over them.

I soon learned that when people asked me how

I was doing, it was more appropriate for me to say "not bad" and quickly turn the corner into another aisle. But I also discovered that when I didn't share the whole truth, I almost immediately started to cry. I found the canned beans aisle about the best section to shed a few tears without being noticed.

Cry Me a River

Crying nearly everywhere is not much fun, but I eventually learned that it's okay. That was very helpful for me, because I did a lot of it. When my vial of dust was moving along the assembly line in heaven, the angel in charge of crying habits was possibly chatting with a co-worker when she accidentally squeezed the eye dropper a little too hard.

I've always heard that the eyes are the window to the soul. I cried so much, I imagined people looking at my red, puffy eyes and saying, "Why doesn't she pull her shades down?"

One of the Hollywood myths is that people look pretty when they cry. Well, maybe so if you're all made up, you're not really upset, and you have put little drops in your eyes to make them tear up. But, nobody looks cute when they're really crying—at least, I don't.

29

When I studied acting, I saw myself on TV once a week over a period of two years. In some of the scenes, I would cry. It was not a pretty sight. Nor did I look romantic. When I cry, my face squidules up. The whites of my eyes get all those red lines like the fake eyes kids buy at Halloween. And sometimes my face even breaks out in a rash.

Right after my separation, I had to discipline myself to keep from crying in public. But holding emotion in all day leaves only the night to let it go. Now we all know that when we are under a lot of stress, rest is particularly important. So I would think, "I'll cry while I'm cooking dinner, have another good cry after dinner while reading some self-help book, and then I'll be ready to sleep when my head hits the pillow." Don't you just love well-thought-out plans?

I'd get all ready for bed, including moisturing my face. I'd lay there and think. Big mistake. The tears would start running down my face like acid rain, through my moisturizer and into my ears—filling them up and then overflowing into my hair. So much for rest. I'd have to get back up, drain my ears, and blot my eyes with a cold rag to keep the swelling down. Great for when you want to wake up. Not so good when you're trying to sleep. It was irritating. I couldn't even be miserable in peace.

I found my car to be a fairly safe place to cry, as long as I didn't do it at a stoplight. I just knew the people in the cars on either side of me were saying, "Look at that very strange lady. She is crying. I can't believe it. You'd think she could save such a thing for the privacy of her own home, instead of embarrassing us like this."

Normally, I cry when I see a dead dog or cat on the road. During this time of ultra-sensitivity, I even cried when I saw a dead skunk. "And why not?" I asked myself. "Skunks are just as deserving of grief as other animals."

Sometimes I get stress headaches when I try to hold back my tears, so I came up with an alternative plan. If I feel tears coming on and there is no place for me to go away from people, I just let the tears flow. If I am asked what is wrong and I don't feel like sharing, I merely say, "My eyes are crying, what can I say?" If making up stories were allowed, I could say, "I have a bug in both eyes." But then I would feel guilty for lying. So, I stick with the truth: it was the angel in heaven—the one in charge of crying habits.

> *"And God will wipe away every tear from their eyes; there shall be no more death, nor sorrow, nor crying; and there shall be no more pain, for the former things have passed away" (Rev. 21:4).*

31

Frustration

There was one thing that caused me a considerable amount of frustration—all the paper work I had to deal with. The attorney wanted copies of all kinds of important papers, most of which I did not have of course. And, there were insurance policies to change and my will.

In addition, there was a lot of paper work involved in closing out a mail-order business that my ex had started, but then left with me. Even if I had wanted to continue to run the business, and I didn't, I had neither the funds to order new products, nor the credit rating as an individual that was necessary.

As irritating as all of this was, I finally did feel that I was making pretty good headway when a bomb dropped. Uncle Sam decided I was due for an audit. The decision was timely.

I had been very careful to save every receipt, and I had hired an accountant even though there wasn't much for him to do except fill out the proper forms. Paying his fee was difficult for me, but I figured that my chances of being audited were much less if a professional filed the forms.

Obviously my safety precautions had not helped. I called my accountant. His secretary informed me that he was out of town and he would not be returning until after my audit appointment. Oh, boy!

I guess things were a little slow around the I.R.S. office because the auditor commented that everyone in the building was looking forward to seeing what happened with my case. I was the first audit of the year. Lucky me! I'd sent in my return well in advance of everyone else—not a good move, I was learning.

I've never heard anyone say they had an enjoyable time being audited. I have to join the ranks of those frustrated individuals. It was extremely trying. The whereabouts of every penny was scrutinized.

Even though I had done nothing wrong, the situation and the manner of questioning made me feel like I must have done something wrong. They were primarily concerned with the fact that my house payments went to an individual rather than a bank. Fortunately, I had every cancelled check I needed to verify the figures on my tax returns.

Although I did have a pretty nice auditor, he made a mistake in his calculations; and for about five minutes, while he checked some resources, I thought I was going to owe money. I cried during those five minutes. But he returned with good news—I didn't owe anything after all.

The two hour experience confirmed the fact

that even though paper work is one of my least favorite chores, it could save me a lot of grief.

I'm hoping that when we get to heaven, the extent of the required paper work will be to sign in.

"And whatever you do, do it heartily, as to the Lord and not to men" (Col. 3:23).

Anger then Fear

Trying to deal with all the emotions that were welling up, overflowing, and just plain making my body and mind a veritable volcano of temperaments was exhausting. Especially when it came to anger.

"Let's see," I would say to myself, "Who should I be angry with? The feeling of outrage is definitely there. Who deserves to receive the verbal rocks that I feel I must hurl? My ex-husband? Excellent choice, but impractical. Myself? I'm good at that, but I've already beaten myself to a pulp with 'if onlys.' God? No way. (I haven't yet learned that God can handle my anger.) Satan? Another appropriate choice, but he would love to see me waste my energy in such an unproductive way."

Then that word came to mind—*forgive.* I had

to remind myself that God did not merely suggest that I forgive, He commanded me to do so. He also said that He would forgive me as I forgave others. Now there's a motivation if I ever heard one.

> *"For if you forgive men their trespasses, your heavenly Father will also forgive you. But if you do not forgive men their trespasses, neither will your Father forgive your trespasses" (Matt. 6:14–15).*

"Okay, I forgive," I said. But I still felt anger and resentment. I needed to do something to let out all those feelings. I started an anger notebook where I wrote down all my feelings. (This kind of paper work, I didn't mind.) I also talked and yelled at the wall, and cried. After all that, I felt somewhat empty—empty until fear moved in and filled up the void.

I imagined how I would fare as a bag lady.

"Here I am, all by myself, divorced, not very young. Who is going to want me? What am I going to do? Can I make it as a single woman financially? Socially? Does God still love me?" Of course God still loved me. But did anyone else? Sure they did—my son, my dog, my relatives, my friends. But would some man find me attractive enough to ask me out? After that, would he find me interesting enough to continue dating me? Who knew?

I got down to the nitty-gritty of my fears. In what I call "toilet-flush thinking," I first imagined myself moving out of my nice little townhouse into a very low-rent district with no garage and many area robberies. From there, I lost most everything I owned to garage—or in this case, no-garage—sales.

Then I imagined how I would fare as a bag lady. At this point, a hint of that old positive thinking I was once known for appeared: "Remember all those items you have seen strewn alongside the freeway? If all else fails, you can furnish your shack with 'early-to-late freeway debris.'" I'd seen sofas, refrigerators, ladders, mattresses, lounge chairs, cushions, and more. It had possibilities. The objects would probably be a bit scuffed up, but so was I.

During this time of exaggerated insecurity, I went to my first job interview in Los Angeles. Loaded with fearful thoughts, including memories of television news reports on crime, I was pretty sure that my car would be stolen, or at least broken into, or that I would be murdered, raped . . . at least robbed. I could not believe it when, once I finished my interview, I walked safely back to my car, which was still there and in one piece. I didn't get the job, but who cared? I still had my car, and, most importantly, I was still alive! I sang praises all the way home.

"And my God shall supply all your need according to His riches in glory by Christ Jesus" (Phil. 4:19).

Fun

I was getting a little anxious about whether or not I'd ever be able to find a decent-paying permanent job. But, since one had not yet come my way, I decided to go to my old home town in Colorado. I had attended The Telluride Film Festival every year since it started in 1974, and I had been a host every year since we started the host program.

I was excited to have the opportunity to be a part of the festival again and to visit relatives and friends. In a town this small, friends are like extended family.

This was my first trip by myself since the divorce, and I can't say that it was all smooth sailing. On the flight from Orange County to Phoenix, the fellow sitting next to me got airsick. I ended up attending to him, as the flight attendants would not get near him. The flight from New Mexico to Telluride, the third leg of the trip, was extremely bumpy, and the little girl sitting next to me also got sick. There were no attendants on this flight, so once again the job was mine. It wouldn't have been so bad, but I'm not wild about flying to begin with. Oh well, it kept my mind off fear.

We had to land in Montrose instead of Telluride because of thunderstorms. That meant an hour wait for a transfer service, and then a long van ride to Telluride. I was glad to finally arrive at my brother and sister-in-law's home, where I stayed for two days, before I checked into the hotel where I stayed during the festival.

In past years, I had been fortunate to host some terrific people—Mr. and Mrs. John Carradine, Mr. and Mrs. Joel McCrea, and Mr. and Mrs. Harry Carey, Jr., to name a few. This year was certainly no exception. I was thrilled when I found out I would be hosting Mr. and Mrs. James Stewart.

It isn't often that you have the opportunity to be in the presence of a living legend. Mr. Stewart was as kind and as genteel a man as you would ever want to meet. It was a pleasure to show him and his lovely wife around during the festival.

It was fun, too, visiting with friends, some of whom I'd been quite close to for many years. Most of them were aware of my divorce, but a few were not. The difficult part was talking to couples who had been close friends of *ours*. One gal spoke excitedly of a building project that she and her husband would be doing with me and my ex-husband. I felt a little uncomfortable as I explained, "Obviously, you haven't heard that we are divorced."

She was surprised, embarrassed, and she apologized profusely. I assured her that it was okay, and quickly changed the subject. It would take awhile for all of us to get used to me as an individual rather than me as one-half of a couple.

After the festival, I had a day and a half to visit with my sister and her family before returning home.

All in all, it was a good trip, and I was very glad I had taken it. I felt a little more confident that there were things I could do and enjoy . . . on my own.

"I can do all things through Christ who strengthens me" (Phil. 4:13).

39

Mental Therapy

"Excuse me, I just had major surgery. Can you heal me?"

One of the most beneficial things I did after the divorce was to participate in some workshops. Two of the most helpful were a divorce recovery workshop and the Beginning Again Workshop. (The Beginning Again Workshops were originated and are led by Terry Hershey. He also authored a book entitled *Beginning Again: Life After a Relationship Ends*).

I learned that I needed to focus not on my misery, but on a constructive plan for my new life. It was comforting to meet others who were feeling similar pain, emotional upheaval, and unusual patterns of behavior. For instance, I had already learned that sharing "war stories" wasn't a good idea, but it was reassuring to know that I wasn't the only one who had done that.

I realized that I could throw out some of the "rocks" that I'd been carrying around in the backpack of my mind. I had been playing the old "if only I'd done this, and hadn't done that, everything would have been different" game. I learned that these "guilt rocks" were not only unnecessary but were slowing my progress.

Once again, I was reminded of the fact that

God had forgiven me. I needed to forgive myself as well as others.

> *"If we confess our sins, He is faithful and just to forgive us our sins and to cleanse us from all unrighteousness" (1 John 1:9).*

Anything for a Quick Fix

"You Name It, We've Got It Video Town, this is George, can I help you?" came the voice through my phone line.

"I hope so. I'd like something in a divorce-workout-tape," I said.

"You mean an exercise video, don't you?" George asked.

"No," I replied, "I mean a video that is like an exercise workout, but it is a workout for people trying to recover from a divorce."

"Sorry, ma'am. We have everything here, and there is no such thing on the market. Maybe you should make one. Good luck," snickered George.

Okay, so I'll have to stick with church, books, audio tapes, radio programs, seminars, lectures, periodic visits to my therapist, and support groups. Actually, that should keep me busy enough.

One thing I was sure that I needed was some

more female friends. I had only a few close friends who lived near me, and I wanted to make friends with some of the ladies from my church.

I wondered how I should go about the process of making new friends. Perhaps I could wear a T-shirt which read: "Female Friend Needed, Apply Here. Requirements: Christian, sharing, caring, respect, sense of humor." Naa. I'm outgoing, but not that bold. Maybe I'd meet some ladies at all the church functions I'd be going to—that way, we'd have something in common. That seemed like a good plan.

The first group I joined after my ex left was a "recovery group." You could be recovering from anything to be a part of this group. And I believe we had a person representing one of every possible thing an individual could need to recover from.

It was different from any group I have ever joined. I'm still confused about whether or not it was helpful for me. The facilitator asked each of us very personal questions. Some of the questions, I later confirmed, were really inappropriate for mixed company. Also, one of the group members shared some of my private information with someone outside our group, which was not only embarrassing, but very painful to have someone betray a trust at a time when I was particularly vulnerable. Everyone in the group had signed a confidentiality paper, but not everyone in the group took it seriously. I had a choice; I could forget all groups based on that experience or try again. I don't give up that easy.

My next adventure was my first women's retreat. It was a very long drive to the retreat site, the traffic was horrendous, and the weather was gloomy. I knew a few ladies, but they were already teamed up with roommates. So, I had a choice to be by myself or to room with some gals I didn't know. Of course, I chose to have roommates. I could see potential friends with this arrangement.

At first, the fact that I did not know my roommates was okay with me. But as it turned out, the four of them were all good buddies, and they were quite a bit younger than I. One of the girls was going to be getting married soon, so I certainly did not feel comfortable sharing my unhappy-ending marriage story. When asked, I gave as brief a synopsis of my situation as possible. They were polite enough, but they did not ask me to join them in anything. So, I was still on my own. At mealtimes, I did make some acquaintances with ladies who were sitting at the same table.

After one of the speaker sessions, we broke up into small groups. The subject had been forgiveness—boy, did I need to hear that one. In my group were a few other gals who had been through what I was going through. When I heard that they had felt as mixed up as I was feeling, I was relieved. It's always comforting to know you are not the only one who ever felt so overwhelmed.

Each group member was allowed time to vent their anger. Then we moved on to discuss those people we needed to forgive. That was a time of cleansing for me.

One of the speakers was a very energetic lady who encouraged anyone who wanted to speak privately to her to do so. I made an appointment for a few minutes of her time. I was quite surprised to learn that she too had survived a divorce. She was encouraging to me, and she gave me her phone number, suggesting that we get together sometime. By all means I would take her up on her offer. A new friend!

The last day of the retreat, the sun came out. Everything was brighter, including my outlook on life.

Our church had some terrific women's seminars. As I participated in these events, fresh from the ravages of divorce, I was encouraged most of the time. But sometimes, I became discouraged.

I'd watch these well-groomed, well-dressed ladies telling the secrets of a happy, successful life. I'd think, *That's easy for them to say. I mean, what problems do they have? They are lovely; probably have a healthy bank account; a loving, supportive husband; darling, perfectly behaved kids; live in a huge, beautiful home.* Who wouldn't feel down with that line of thinking? I was obviously having a pity party at these times, but it was hard to identify with many of the speakers.

I needed to keep my eyes on God, not on the mess I was in.

There was, however, one lady who really got through to me during a seminar. Not only had she survived a divorce but she also had a physical handicap. She was not a professional speaker, but she looked confident and dressed just as nicely as all the other speakers. What set her apart was that she spoke from her heart. She explained that even though she experienced some hard times, she was doing fine because she relied on Jesus for her strength. Now, this certainly was not the first time I had heard that. But when she said it, the way she said it, the point got through to me. I needed to keep my eyes on God, not on the mess I was in.

I noticed, while attending these seminars and groups, that nearly everyone had day-planner notebooks. I don't usually follow the crowd just to be following the crowd. But if everyone had one of these, then I figured I should get one. I looked at some of the department stores, but the cost was prohibitive. No problem, I just waited until I found one on sale. I was so excited. Then I opened it up and saw all those blank lines. Filling them in might be tough. "Hmmm . . . not much going on that I want to write in such an official-looking book. Appointments with the attorney? No, that reminds me of the divorce. Job interviews? No, there were not enough of those to waste starting the book. Dates? Ha Ha!"

"Okay, this is silly," I continued talking to myself. "Look at your wall calendar, and transfer that stuff into the book. Take one month for example. Let's see. Dental appointment. Clean cobwebs off ceiling in my room. Sprinkle the yard with snail bite. Meeting at church. Pay bills. Spray the daisy plant for aphids. Hair cut. Make an appointment with a psychologist—boy, I hope so, with a social calendar like that. Until my appointments get a little more exciting, I think I'll just leave them on the one-inch squares on my wall calendar. They fit better. Besides, how embarrassing would it be to lose that day-planner at one of these seminars! Whoever found it would have to open it up to see who it belonged to. Papers would not fall out of it, markers would not slip, there would not be arrows pointing elsewhere because of lack of writing space. No. I can't do it. I'll have to wait."

"And do not be conformed to this world, but be transformed by the renewing of your mind, that you may prove what is that good and acceptable and perfect will of God" (Rom. 12:2).

CHAPTER THREE

Invalid Stage: How About Some Crutches

Having Paul half the time was a lot better than having him none of the time, but it wasn't easy to get used to. And it still hurts.

With no other adult around, I was tempted to share my woes with Paul. But when the problems related to the divorce, as most of them did, I tried not to burden him. That left Taffy, our dog. When she was asleep, she was a great listener. Otherwise, her attention span was pretty limited. It's embarrassing to have a dog walk away from you, especially during a heavy moment.

As long as Paul and Taffy were with me, things were okay—we were still a little family. But every Wednesday evening and every other weekend, they went to his dad's house. And that first year, they went for the whole summer.

Even now, every time Paul moves out for his six months at his "other house," my emotions quiver and my insides feel as if they are being scraped out with a potato peeler.

The pain runs deep
It stings my eyes
It lumps in my throat
It aches in my chest
My heart cries out to God—Why?

The sadness I felt because of these separations was compounded by the Little League games I watched him play. When Paul was at his dad's, I drove to the games by myself. When I got there, I watched Paul play by myself, and when they were over, I drove home by myself.

When I was married, my ex-husband and I had to take separate cars to a game at times; now, we were taking separate lives. Suddenly, we had only two things in common—memories and our son.

I sat in the stands to watch the games, but I couldn't help watching the "together" families around me. In most cases, I was able to hold back the tears until my ride home. But, sometimes, at night games, when there were no people sitting near me, I'd let the tears flow.

**I couldn't help watching the
"together" families around me.**

I really felt lost without Paul. I believed that I needed to be taking care of him, but I couldn't do that when he wasn't with me. It was a very helpless feeling, and I didn't know how to deal with it.

> *"I cried to the LORD with my voice,*
> *And He heard me from His holy hill.*
> *Selah*
> *I lay down and slept;*
> *I awoke, for the LORD sustained me"*
> *(Ps. 3:4–5).*

Family Matters

When Paul was with me, I got caught up in a syndrome well known to single parents. It's the old how-can-I-keep-my-child-loving-me-when-his-other-house-can-give-him-more-fun-and-toys game. I began to exam my parenting style to see what changes might be appropriate.

Of Paul's two parents, he considered me to be the strict one, so I figured for starters, I could lighten up a little bit. One morning, I gave Paul his vitamin pill as usual. Many times in the past, the pill had ended up in his coat pocket, behind the sofa, at the end of an ant trail from the front door, in the wastebasket, or on the table hidden under some papers. But on this day, instead of pestering him to take it, I just watched as he lay on his back on the floor and threw it up in the air and tried to catch it in his mouth.

Unfortunately, Taffy was trying to accomplish the same feat. Guess who succeeded? Oh well, so the dog is healthier!

On Mother's Day, Paul wanted to make cookies. He had helped me before, but this time he wanted to make them all by himself. My strict side wanted to say no, but my new, looser personality managed to win out.

It was harder than I thought not to help him, especially when he started throwing the cookie batter into the air like pizza dough. I had to bite my tongue when it hit the glass lamp shade. Not only would I have to eat cookies with dust in them but I would be forced to clean the lamp shade.

There comes a time, however, when good-natured silliness runs into the brick wall of mischief. One day, when I was in a hurry to get ready for an interview, I opened up the cap on my toothpaste, as I had done without mishap a few million other times (other than that one time when I brushed my teeth with hair-styling gel). But this time when I squeezed the tube, out came water. I squeezed again. Very watered-down toothpaste slopped out. I didn't have time to figure it out, so I ran into Paul's bathroom, only to find his toothpaste in the same condition. Two tubes ruined! When I confronted Paul that afternoon, he informed me that it was a self-initiated science experiment. What do you say to the budding scientist? "Please don't ever do that again."

For some time during the heat of the divorce, my mind just wasn't focused on my household duties. And just as I was beginning to feel secure again in my ability to remember to check pants pockets for candy, gum, wrappers, pennies, toys, animals, uneaten snacks, notes, I had a new experience. I opened the washer lid at the end of the cycle to find what looked like a washed playing card. On further observation, I found out it was actually an entire deck of playing cards. How in the world could that have slipped by?

"It was a miniature deck and it was in the back pocket, Mom."

What do you say to the budding magician specializing in card tricks? Once again, I relied on the obvious: "Please try to remember to remove items from your pockets." At least this incident inspired me to double-check all pockets more carefully. And I did learn a helpful hint: Clean up washed cards while the mess is still wet. If you wait for them to dry, they turn into hardened cement and require a putty knife to get them off the side and bottom of the washer.

Pets: Arrivals and Departures

I believe Paul felt that we would be more of a family if we had more family members. I could sympathize with his feelings. Lacking the possibility of obtaining any instant siblings, more pets seemed the appropriate solution. We went through a number of them.

First there was the hamster we had to return because he turned out to be a biter. I took an unexpected trip to the emergency ward for a tetanus shot after demonstrating to Paul the correct way to pick up the furry little critter.

**Fish were too hard on my
emotions.**

Paul then decided a fish would be less dangerous. It was, but it only lived for two weeks. Paul laughed at me when I cried. We went to a different pet store to buy our second fish. This one lasted longer—about two-and-one-half weeks. As it turned out, I had taken care of it too well. The guy at the pet store had told us that the cleaner we kept the water, the longer the fish would live. He'd forgotten to tell us that we were supposed to leave some of the old water in the bowl so the change wouldn't be too much of a shock to the fish's system. Since it was the salesperson's error, we were eligible to receive a replacement fish for free, but I declined. Fish were too hard on my emotions.

I had barely recovered from the pain of accidentally killing the fish when Paul came home from school with a mouse. One of the girls in his science class had brought it to school. Her parents had insisted she find another home for it—smart parents. Paul couldn't resist, and he knew I couldn't either, once I understood that we were the only ones who could save this creature from being put to sleep or fed to a snake. I even voted for the latter, until he explained that this particular mouse was the young lady's favorite pet.

It wasn't long before Paul talked me into getting another mouse to keep the first mouse company. It didn't occur to us that one might be a female and the other a male. They did indeed keep each other company. They proceeded to have a ton of babies. If you have ever smelled mice, you will know why my son decided to let the entire family go free in a field behind his dad's house.

Next came the snake. The pet store where we got it guaranteed the health of their pets for thirty days. Our snake lived forty-five days. I couldn't believe how much I cried over a snake, especially one that lived on cute little fish. However, in the almost-good-news department, there was one little fish remaining. We had saved him because he was so different—an albino. You could see right through him. No longer a potential snake snack, he grew very fat. But after a while he stopped eating and still remained fat. One day he expelled a bunch of junk on the bottom of his bowl.

Applying my new knowledge of fish care, I cleaned the bowl and left some of the old water and some of the above-mentioned questionable material in the bowl. That was good, because the strange stuff turned out to be twenty-eight baby fish (I counted). *He* was not the proper title for this proud parent! The sad part was that every one of them eventually died—including mom.

Can you believe that Paul had the nerve to ask for another pet? Perhaps he would have been less eager for another animal if I'd put him in charge of pet burials; but as the new head of the household, I assumed that responsibility was mine. It was not my favorite job. I stood firm—family growth or no family growth, I could not handle any more deaths. My grief was nearly killing me.

> *"Are not two sparrows sold for a copper coin? And not one of them falls to the ground apart from your Father's will.*
> *But the very hairs of your head are all numbered.*
> *Do not fear therefore; you are of more value than many sparrows" (Matt. 10:29–31).*

Morality Lesson

Despite my plan to lighten up a little, I still felt strongly the need to impart Christian morals to Paul in a world where he was constantly bombarded with immorality. Since I had no authority over Paul when he wasn't with me, I felt I needed to monitor more carefully what he read, saw, and listened to when he was with me.

Despite my plans to lighten up a little, I still felt strongly the need to impart Christian morals to Paul.

One afternoon, I came home from the market after Paul had arrived home from school. He was sitting at the dining room table with his back to me. As I was setting down the groceries, I said, "Hi." He didn't respond, so I repeated myself in a louder voice. Still nothing.

Then I noticed that he had on headphones, so I walked around in front of him and waved my arms as I said, "Hello!"

Finally, he said, "Hi, Mom."

"What are you listening to?" I asked.

"A tape that Mark let me borrow," he answered.

"You know that it's not a good idea to listen to music while you're doing your homework," I said. We'd had this conversation before.

"Mom, it's okay. This stuff is super easy."

"You read the study guide that you brought home from school. This isn't just my idea, you know."

"Please?" he whined.

"No. Sorry."

"Okay," he gave in. "But can I just listen to this last song? It's my favorite."

"What kind of music is this? Is it weird or perverted?"

"No," he answered in an injured tone.

"Okay," I said. "But, just that one song."

That being settled, I headed back to the

kitchen to put away the groceries. I heard Paul tapping his pencil rhythmically on the table, and then I heard him singing in rap-style, "Let's go get some drugs, then we'll get some girls, then we'll get high . . ."

I ran back to the table and snatched the head phones off his head. Paul started laughing like crazy.

"I'm sure, Mom! I was just kidding!" he said.

"Well, it's not funny," I told him, reading the unoffensive words of the song. (Later I laughed—when he wasn't around.)

We were both happy: I, because he was doing his homework without music; and he, because he got my goat.

CHAPTER FOUR

Single
Parenting

Bonding

Much of what I read on the subject of single parenting indicated that parent-child bonding was especially important during this post-divorce adjustment. Paul felt the loss of our family unit, too; he needed to feel secure that he was still of utmost importance to me even though my lifestyle was changing. Someone suggested that I take him on a vacation, and I decided to go for it.

I let Paul choose where we would go. I figured he's pick Sea World for a couple of days or maybe San Francisco for a weekend. No such luck. He wanted to go to the World Expo in Canada.

I didn't discover until after I promised we would go that the trip was not going to be cheap. I failed to consider that the airline companies and the hotel chains might take full advantage of the popularity of the event. I also failed to consider how many other people had decided to take the same trip. Airline tickets and a place to stay were almost impossible to come by, even at the highest rates. But I persevered. Nothing could keep me from arranging this bonding-on-vacation experience.

**I had never planned a trip as a
single parent.**

I borrowed some money, got the plane tickets, and called a special phone number in Canada to arrange a stay at a temporary bed-and-breakfast.

I had never planned a trip as a single parent, so I was anxious to do everything right. About a week before the flight, I picked up the tickets from the travel agent. I read weather reports in order to pack proper clothing (and, just in case, I packed clothing for weather that wasn't in the forecasts). I was still a little nervous, but I shared Paul's excitement as we drove to the airport to catch our plane.

My excitement began to wane once we got to the airport. After parking the car and lugging our bags to the terminal, we waited at the check-in counter, where a lady informed us that our tickets had been written incorrectly and were, therefore, invalid. Unfortunately, she said, the flight was completely full.

I was beginning to work up to a full panic when the ticket counter lady saved me. "Wait. There are, in fact, two seats open, and I can rewrite these tickets for you." (Once on the plane, we couldn't help but notice that there were quite a few empty seats. But we didn't care. We were on our way.)

Once in Canada, we had a choice between a taxi and a bus to get to our destination. After checking out the fares, I picked the bus. The lady who took our money said we just had to tell our driver where we wanted to go—that sounded easy enough. When the driver dropped us off, he said the address we wanted was just down the street a bit. It wasn't. We sat on our luggage at an intersection, and waved at every taxi that went past. The drivers merely waved back at us.

Paul and I tried to figure out if maybe there was a different signal for hailing cabs in Canada. We experimented. Nothing seemed to work, but we had fun.

After about half an hour, a taxi finally stopped, and we made it to our destination. The house left a little to be desired: there were four very small guest rooms located on the bottom floor of a two-story dwelling. There was only one bathroom for all the guests, and the only towels appeared to have already been used. Rita, our hostess, assured us that we wouldn't need a key—she and her husband were *always* at home. Despite the poor first impression, we were ready to make the most of the situation—we paid for the accommodations in advance, after all, and were there only to sleep. That night, however, we learned that the floor above us creaked; it was a long night.

For the next few days, we encountered numerous frustrations at the B and B, or "Bummer and Bummer," as we called it. One morning, I went to use the bathroom, and the toilet was out of order. Rita reluctantly let me use hers. Another morning, there were no towels or soap for our showers. I sent Paul upstairs to get some, and he came back with two towels and a dripping wet, soggy bar of soap—Rita hadn't been able to find any, so she went into her bathroom, took the bar out of her own shower, and plunked it into his hand. After Paul and I got over the shock, we laughed like crazy.

One particularly hot day, we headed "home" from the Expo completely exhausted and ready for bed. We arrived at Rita's at 8:00 P.M. We knocked on the door; no answer. We knocked again and again; still, no answer. We walked around to the back of the house; no answer. We searched under mats for the key. We did everything we could think of to try to get into the house, with the exception of breaking into it (although that thought did run through our minds).

Finally, I knocked on the door of the house to the left of our B and B. Those folks said they were sorry but they did not have a key, nor did they know where Rita and her hubby were. We tried the house on the right side. An elderly lady who spoke little English came to the door. She turned out to be Rita's mom, and I thought we had hit pay dirt, but no such luck. She told us that Rita used to leave her a key, but not anymore. Then she closed the door.

Paul and I stood there dumbfounded, but before we could move, the door opened again. This time it was Rita's sister. She spoke good English, and she invited us into the house to wait for Rita to return.

Once inside, I inquired as to Rita's whereabouts. Sis explained that Rita and her husband had gone to dinner and a play. How nice for them. But at least Sis was hospitable. She offered us iced tea, and she invited us to watch a TV movie with them.

At 10:30 P.M., Rita and husband finally showed up. We said our good-byes to Sis, Mom, and the other relatives who had joined us for the movie, and we overlooked Rita's lack of apology.

*"Yet in all these things we are more than
conquerors through Him who loved us"
(Rom. 8:37).*

Forewarned about the lines at the Expo, we
weren't disappointed. We saw some great things
and met some nice people while waiting in the
lines. The best show we saw was a 3-D nature
film worth the three hours of waiting it took to
get in.

We teamed up, for one day of Expoing, with a
very nice young man that Paul and I had be-
friended on the airplane. I was very pleased that
he wanted to go on the amusement rides with
Paul (I don't find the rides amusing). So, Paul had
company and I was able to watch from the safety
of solid ground.

We took one-and-a-half days to see some of the
other tourist attractions in the area. We checked
out the historic part of downtown Vancouver for
half a day, and the day before we left Canada, we
went to Victoria by ferry. Our favorite sights on
that lovely island were the Butchart Gardens
and the victorian buildings of downtown. Rain
had been predicted for the day but blue skies pre-
vailed, and we had a particularly nice time.

Paul and I really enjoyed our trip, mishaps and
all. We'd had plenty of time to talk about all
kinds of things, serious and silly. Our adven-
tures at Rita's gave us some great stories and

some unforgettable memories. Most importantly, we had a bonding experience shared by
just the two of us—we felt closer to one another.
Our time together, away from the daily grind,
gave us the opportunity to further develop our
relationship as mother and son as well as our
friendship as individuals who enjoy each other.

Fast Points

As a single mother, I became aware of a simple
task I'd never done. Paul was always trying to
talk me into taking him to McDonald's drive-
thru. We had been there a few times before, but
never with me in the driver's seat. However, I decided this could earn some points for me in the
"cool parent" department. How difficult could it
be, after all? I found out.

The drive-thru area of the McDonald's we
went to was a little confusing—for me, anyway. I
drove around the back and headed for the window. Paul, trying to remain calm, said, "Mom,
you just passed the speaker."

"Oh," I said, embarrassed. I had to back up
fast, before the car behind us got to the speaker.
Then I made another mistake—I yelled our order
into the box. Paul and a voice from within the
box said in unison, "You don't have to yell!"
Sheepishly, I finished ordering in a quieter voice.

71

Then I proceeded to the window. I paid the money. The attendant asked, "What kind of a drink do you want with your Happy Meal?"

I replied that I hadn't ordered a Happy Meal.

As Paul moaned and hid his head in his hands, she said, "I wasn't speaking to you. I was talking to the people in the car behind you." Too late, I noticed the microphone.

I sat there expectantly for a few seconds before Paul asked what I was waiting for. "The food," I told him in surprise. This was all he could take. "Mom," he groaned, "you have to drive up to the *next* window to get the food! This window is just for paying."

Paul reprimanded me for the next few miles while I defended my integrity. After all, if you have never done something like that, how are you supposed to know? So much for "cool parent" points.

The next time I had an occasion to pick up a fast-food snack for Paul, he chose not to go with me. I decided it was safer to walk in and order at the counter. But I was puzzled when the fellow set an empty cup in front of me. I finally asked him about it and he explained that there was a drink dispenser where I could serve myself. When I went to it, though, there were just a few ice cubes lying on the overflow tray. So I asked if I could get some ice. The fellow came over and showed me that you could press the cup up against a metal handle, and—voila! out came ice cubes. I mentioned to him, in defense, that they might want to mark that dispenser with the word *Ice*. He, however, simply snickered and looked at me with a clear, nonverbal message that said, "You are the only person in the whole world who does not already know this, and that includes foreigners and aliens from outer space." (I explained to him that I did not frequent fast-food establishments. But, the look on his face didn't change.)

Boy, was I glad that Paul had not come with me! At first, I wasn't going to share my experience with him, but then I changed my mind. Why not give him something to chuckle about? He finds my bloopers amusing, as long as he isn't with me. It's good for him to laugh, and it's good for me to laugh.

> *"A merry heart does good, like medicine,*
> *But a broken spirit dries the bones"*
> *(Prov. 17:22).*

A Different Kind of Trial

A more difficult aspect of single parenting was having to face alone with Paul some of the trials in his life. Paul was born with a swallowing disorder. From the time he started drinking mom's milk, he threw up a lot, and when he was old enough to eat solid foods, he ate very slowly. When he was five, food started to get stuck in his esophagus; sometimes, he was able to dislodge it within a few minutes, and other times it took hours. I always prayed for him at such times, and I would rub his back as he tried to get the food out. Fortunately, I would remain calm and try to encourage him, but I always felt so helpless. No physician we took him to was able to diagnose, let alone remedy, the problem.

On Paul's ninth birthday, he had to be admitted into the hospital because he had a piece of food stuck in his esophagus that he was unable to get out by himself. Our doctor decided to put Paul to sleep and look down his esophagus with a scope to see first hand what was causing the problem. Afterward, he explained that Paul's esophagus was extremely narrow at one spot. In the process of looking down there, the doctor had dilated the esophagus a little, but he suggested we see a specialist.

Things went well with Paul for quite some time, but when he was eleven—divorce time— he started having problems again. After searching for almost a year, we finally found a doctor who not only knew his business (pediatric gastroenterology!), but was also a neat guy.

After the doctor reviewed Paul's x-rays, which showed nothing, he informed us that it would be necessary for Paul to come to the hospital to have some specific tests. He would do one series to check what kind of pressure, or peristalsis, Paul had in his esophagus while he was swallowing.

The doctor and the group of nurses who worked with him at the hospital were great. Each one had a good sense of humor, which made the experience less stressful for both Paul and me. But it was still no fun for Paul: the test involved the doctor pushing and pulling a tube up and down Paul's esophagus while he counted to five.

"You do remember how to count to five and back, don't you?" the doctor asked.

Without a moment's pause, Paul came back with, "Sure, but will you understand me when I do?"

The doctor blushed, and the nurses and I roared with laughter. I was so glad that the Lord had given Paul a good sense of humor.

Paul made it through the tedious testing process, but the results didn't give us an answer. We would have to go back for more—this time a dilation of his esophagus.

Paul was living at his dad's during this time, so I chose a Wednesday, my midweek day with Paul, for the next test. That way he could also spend the evening with me.

This procedure was harder to sit through. The shot to lessen the pain was the easy part. The rest was almost unbearable.

When the drugs had taken effect, the doctor stuck an instrument down Paul's throat that enabled him to see inside. He even took a photograph. It sounds simple enough, but throughout the process, Paul moaned and groaned in pain, complaining that he could not breathe. The nurse assured me it was a false sensation. I prayed that they all knew what they were doing.

> *"Be strong and of good courage, do not fear nor be afraid of them; for the* LORD *your God, He is the One who goes with you. He will not leave you nor forsake you"* (Deut. 31:6).

When the doctor arrived at the area of constriction, he found that Paul's esophagus was so small that he had to use the smallest of surgical tubes to get through—the kind used in the esophagi of newborn babies.

The nurse had to keep telling Paul to swallow, because, in his drugged state, he kept trying to spit out the tube. He flailed around so much that most of the time it took three of us to hold him still. With both of my hands busy, I couldn't wipe away the tears that ran down my cheeks.

"What's wrong?" the doctor asked.

"I just hate to see him have to go through all of this."

"He won't remember anything," he assured me.

I thought to myself, "But he is experiencing major discomfort right now. I'm feeling pain with him. And I will remember, even if he doesn't." This was a hard time for Mom.

This was a hard time for Mom.

When it was over, they let Paul sleep so that the drugs could wear off, but as soon as we got home, Paul got sick to his stomach. When I called the doctor, he guessed that Paul was allergic to the drugs they had given him. He assured me that Paul would feel better when the drugs wore off completely. I also called Paul's dad. He agreed that Paul should spend the night with me. As it turned out, the drugs did not wear off until the following morning. I was up with him all night.

In the past, I had taken Paul to a hospital by

myself, and many times I had been up all night with him by myself. But this was the first time I didn't have someone else to talk to about what was going on with Paul, or with me. This time I felt particularly alone.

Paul felt great the next day when I had to take him to his dad's house. I called later to see how he was doing, and he was sure he was finally cured. He had just eaten a whole box of popcorn without a single problem. I told him I did not think that popcorn was the right kind of food to be eating just yet. (The doctor agreed when I told him about it, but he was glad to hear that Paul even felt like trying popcorn.)

At our final appointment with the doctor, he told us that Paul really should go through at least one more, possibly two more, dilations, but that the decision was up to us. I asked Paul what he thought, and there was no question in his mind—"No way!"

It was hard not being able to have Paul live with me year round, but it was even harder at times like this. I had to remind myself, again, that even though I wasn't able to be in control of the situation, God was always in complete control of every situation.

"Peace I leave with you, My peace I give to you; not as the world gives do I give to

you. Let not your heart be troubled, neither let it be afraid" (John 14:27).

Don't Send a Card—Take Me Along

I so much wanted our holidays to be special, especially Christmas, but that was difficult with such limited funds. That first Christmas I purchased what Paul called our "Charlie Brown Christmas tree." It wasn't really all that bad, but it wasn't tall and full, like the tree at his dad's house. It didn't have new decorations, nor did it have masses of beautifully wrapped gifts stacked underneath it.

Since Paul had two weeks off for Christmas vacation, he spent one with me and one with his dad. I had him the first week, and he was very eager to get to his dad's house. I was hurt by this, but who could blame him? He said it felt more like a family over there, because there were more people—his dad, an older stepbrother, a new baby stepbrother, and a stepmother. I explained to Paul that a family was a family, no matter how many people were part of it, but inside, I had trouble believing that myself.

As I dropped Paul off at his father's house, I felt overwhelmed with sadness. As I watched him enter the house, I felt left out. I sort of wished that I could have joined them. Fortunately I would not be alone on that Christmas day. Still, it wouldn't be the same.

"The LORD is near to those who have a broken heart" (Ps. 34:18a).

Even though a considerable amount of time has passed, not having Paul live with me full-time continues to be one of the hardest things for me. Making arrangements for holidays and dividing time between two households can get very complicated, but it's the emotional ramifications that are most difficult for me to deal with.

When Paul leaves for a vacation or an extended weekend with his other family, he tells me how exciting it is going to be. Not only do I feel bad that I won't be there to watch him or participate with him in the fun; there are still times when I feel left out.

Half the time I experience what I call a "postcard version" of Paul's life. I get glimpses of the time he spends away from me, but never a complete picture, and that hurts.

Circumstances, of course, are the main problem, but there are other factors too. I am a detail-oriented female. Paul is a headline-oriented male. He is also an adolescent, and trying to get information from an adolescent is like trying to get a child-proof cap off a bottle of medicine. The harder you try, the more frustrated you get, and still the cap stays on.

Paul went on a week-long ski trip with his dad to the town where we used to live. Naturally, when Paul returned I was excited to hear all about it.

"So, how was your trip?" I asked, meaning, of course, "How were the flights, the snow conditions, the weather? Who did you see? Did you have fun?"

His reply was, "Fine."

I waited a few minutes in case he was just catching his breath. No such luck.

"That's it?" I tried again.

"Yep," came his answer.

As time went by, he did share more information with me, but not all that I would have liked. It certainly wasn't the same as if I'd been with him. I won't be in some of the pictures that are taken to be shared for memory's sake later on. But, I am, and will remain, in God's "big picture."

This whole new program of single parenting and part-time mothering was much more difficult than I could ever have imagined it would be, and I didn't like it at all. There were so many plans and dreams that I'd had for Paul and me that fell within the framework of a two-parent family. Now, I wasn't sure how many of those plans or dreams would come true. I was sure of one thing—I needed to keep my eyes focused on God.

> *"But seek first the kingdom of God and His righteousness, and all these things shall be added to you" (Matt. 6:33).*

A Question of Custody

"Hi, Chris, this is Doc."

"Well, what a pleasant surprise to hear from you, Doc."

"I know how busy you are. You did receive the final installment on my bill, didn't you?"

"Yes, thanks. That's not why I'm calling."

"Oh?"

"Unfortunately, you may be required to have more surgery."

"Why? I don't understand."

"We may have to do a complete childectomy."

"No way! You can't be serious. Everything is going as well as can be expected with the current arrangement."

"I wish it wasn't true, but it's here in the court papers."

"Why?"

"Your ex-husband filed the papers through his attorney."

"Simple as that, huh? He can do that, even when there is no cause?"

"I'm afraid so."

"What can I do?"

"I suggest you get an attorney and fight against the request."

"You better believe I'll fight. I don't like being a part-time mom, as it is; there is no way I'll consent to being a no-time mom. Thanks for calling, Doc. I'll talk to you later."

I was outraged! I cried, of course. I said some almost bad words—okay, some genuinely bad words. Of all the crummy things to try to do, especially right before Christmas!

I allowed myself to finish with the fit I was having and then tried to come up with a rational plan—it took a while.

It looked like the attorney game, and, although I didn't want to get into that again, I was willing to do whatever it took. I believed there had to be a kind, understanding, good attorney out there somewhere. A friend from my church gave me the name of an attorney who, to my relief, was able to take the case if I needed her after the initial hearing (at which lawyers weren't allowed.)

"For He Himself has said, 'I will never leave you nor forsake you.' So we may

boldly say: 'The LORD is my helper; I will not fear. What can man do to me?'" (Heb. 13:5–6).

The hearing date found me feeling poorly with a lingering cold-flu combo. I had laryngitis so bad, my voice was barely audible. But I knew I had at least two significant facts in my favor: Paul wanted to continue spending equal time with both parents and our current arrangement had been working fine for almost a year.

"Therefore I take pleasure in infirmities, in reproaches, in needs, in persecutions, in distresses, for Christ's sake. For when I am weak, then I am strong" (2 Cor. 12:10).

I waited forty minutes in the courthouse hall for my ex to show up. It was interesting and unsettling to watch the other ex-couples waiting to be assigned a social worker to hear their cases. Some were chatting amiably as if in line for a ride at a fun park. Others were flirting with each other; still others were sitting stone-faced at opposite ends of the hall benches. A few of these folks said nasty things about their ex-mates in voices loud enough to be heard by everyone in the hall.

Ten minutes after my ex checked in, our social worker walked us to her little hearing room. It was a grueling experience. My laryngitis precluded any screaming I felt like doing. Even my indignant sighs and groans came out as unintimidating squeaks. By the end of our session I was drained. Worse, the woman said that it would be necessary for her to talk with Paul.

Even my indignant sighs and groans came out as unintimidating squeaks.

I had a miserable ride home. I knew Paul did not want to have to go to court, and I didn't want him to have to go through such an experience either. But there was nothing I could do about it, except pray, pray, and pray.

> *"But let all those rejoice who put their trust in You; let them ever shout for joy, because You defend them; let those also who love Your name be joyful in You" (Ps. 5:11).*

I felt good about the Lord defending me, but rejoicing through all of this was tough. Actually, I spent most of the rest of that day crying and praying. I also called friends and relatives and asked for their prayers.

> *"Oh, turn to me, and have mercy on me!*
> *Give Your strength to Your servant, and save*
> *the son of Your maidservant. Show me a*
> *sign for good, that those who hate me may*
> *see it and be ashamed, because You, LORD,*
> *have helped me and comforted me" (Ps.*
> *86:16–17).*

Late that afternoon, I finally felt a real peace within. Just a little while later, Paul called. He had spoken at length with his dad, and we were going to be able to avoid the court battle. I was so excited!

What a relief to know that our equal time arrangement would remain as it was. After all, Paul would not be home all that much longer, anyway. He'd be off to college before I knew it, and I wanted as much time as I could possibly have with him before then.

God had brought me through yet another fiery trial. I was not unsinged, but I was alive and feeling the joy of the Lord within me.

> *"For this day is holy to our LORD. Do not*
> *sorrow, for the joy of the LORD is your*
> *strength" (Neh. 8:10b).*

CHAPTER FIVE

Are You Lonesome Tonight?

When Paul and Taffy left for their half-year stay with Paul's dad, I was left with an empty house—a prematurely empty nest. That's when the loneliness really set in.

It was my turn to have Paul every other weekend and on Wednesday nights. Sometimes during our mid-week visits we went out for dinner, and it became obvious that I was not the only single parent out here. As I saw so many other single parents having that same mid-week visit, I would painfully reflect on the vast numbers of broken homes, and often broken lives. On my way home after one of those visits, I'd usually cry. And I'd pray for Paul and me and for all the other used-to-be-families.

When Paul was not with me, I tried to look at the advantages. There was no one messing up the house, fewer dishes to do, less laundry, less noise . . . but this line of reasoning was not comforting. After all, if I'm the only one in the house, what's my excuse if it's not immaculate? And who wants to cook a nice dinner if there's no one to eat it with? It seems to take forever to dirty enough clothes by myself to fill up the washing machine.

Silence may be golden, but not if that's all you hear. Those six months confirmed something I'd thought all along—hermit-style living is not for me.

Silence may be golden, but not if that's all you hear.

I began to long for human contact, to the point where even junk mail started to look good. I couldn't wait for the mail to arrive every day. Bills were less welcome than they had ever been, but all that meaningless stuff—now that was something. I especially liked the envelopes that had *Personal* printed on them. That made me feel wanted. By some computer printout service, you say? Hey, when you're that lonely, you'll take what you can get!

Sometimes in the early evening I would take a walk around the neighborhood in order to clear my head, keep the blood circulating, and enjoy a little of the wonder of nature. It would have been a good idea if it hadn't been for people.

Smiling couples, walking hand in hand, often had the nerve to walk past me. Families, mom and dad, kids and dog, insisted upon playing and laughing right alongside my path. And, to top it off, folks had barbecues in their backyards, unmindful that not only were their festive noises drifting over their fences, but so was the aroma of their sizzling steaks and hot dogs. How those experiences could ruin my nature walks, as I returned to an empty house and a soggy-from-tears tuna sandwich!

One weekend, I was so lonely I cleaned the stove. Thirty seconds into that project, I knew I needed psychological counseling. No one in their right mind should need to be that busy.

Cheap Fun

The question of what to do for cheap fun on a weekend came up a number of times, even when Paul was with me. One Friday night, we decided the solution was to rent a movie. We decided on a comedy—there was enough tragedy in real life. Including what happened when we got to the checkout counter.

The young girl chewing gum behind the counter asked me the stock questions: name, address, phone number, driver's license number, major credit card number . . . That's where we hit the snag. I didn't even have a minor credit card number to give her.

"We have to have a major credit card number," she repeated. "Why don't you have one?"

I lowered my voice, as I explained, "I just went through a divorce, and I haven't been able to get one of my own yet."

She waited for the large bubble she'd blown to pop. She didn't lower her voice when she answered.

"Yeah? Bummer. My folks got a divorce, too. But, no card, no video."

As I was about to turn and weave my humiliated self through the crowd, another female employee came up behind the counter. "Is there a problem?" she asked.

The young gal announced, "She doesn't have a credit card. Can't get one. She just got divorced."

If there was anyone left in the store who had not yet heard the whole story, they now had. But lady number two was sympathetic. She looked over my information and asked whether anyone in our neighborhood might have a card at that store.

I didn't know anyone, but Paul did, the family of one of his friends. So, he gave their name, and the sympathetic lady said, "We'll use their card as a reference. Sort of a backup in case anything happens."

I didn't think that was a good idea without first asking the people, but I agreed anyway. After all that, there was no way I was going to leave that place empty-handed.

Anonymous Friends

Although getting the mail was a highlight of many of my days, I was becoming annoyed with receiving mail addressed to Mr. and Mrs. I also did not like receiving phone calls that started out with Mrs. I wasn't a Mrs. anymore. It was time to establish my single-person identity.

I decided to call or write everyone I could think of who should be aware of the name change, and announce that I was taking back my maiden name. To my surprise, it wasn't a bad way to make friends. Some of the most encouraging and lively conversations I had were with representatives of utility companies, most of whom were women.

For their records, they all needed to know why I was reporting a name change, and when I told them, they were sympathetic and supportive. Once in a while, I even did some encouraging. It was a different experience sharing stories with people I'd most likely never meet in person—the anonymity added to the openness. Every conversation I had with these ladies was pleasant.

> *"Blessed be the God and Father of our Lord Jesus Christ, the Father of mercies and God of all comfort, who comforts us in all our tribulation, that we may be able to comfort those who are in any trouble, with the comfort with which we ourselves are comforted by God" (2 Cor. 1:3–4).*

Singles' Club

My phone-call friends were great, but I could have made some in-person friends if I had had $400 to spare. I received lots of literature from local singles' clubs. (My guess is they send scouts down to the county courthouse to get the names of people who have filed for divorce. I think of it as the shark technique: they watch for the blood and, while the prey is still freshly injured and weak, they attack.)

One evening, an aggressive, and probably hungry, employee of one of these clubs called me. He asked if I had a few minutes. I had more than a few—it was a Friday night. (This is another part of the shark technique: They call when the average popular person is out on a date, knowing that you are aware of this also, and that you're likely to be more keenly aware of your desperate state.)

This fellow went through the normal introductory chit-chat to make me feel comfortable before the pertinent questions.

"Are you married or in a permanent relationship?"

"I once was, but no."

"What do you do for a living?"

"I'm closing out a small mail-order business. I'm also a model, an actress, and a writer."

"Aha, a model!" He thought he'd hit the jackpot. "Do you have one of *those* modeling pictures?"

"I do have pictures. I don't know if any of them are *those.*"

"That would be great for our files. Do you have children living at home?"

"Yes, a son."

"What are your favorite sports?"

"Swimming, biking, skiing, tennis, walking, sailing."

"That is terrific!" He went on to tell me about their club. It sounded pretty good—big parties in large, beautiful homes, small after-work mixers . . . He explained about the video library where club members could go to view tapes to see who they might want to ask out. I was lonely enough to be interested, but not lonely enough to forget the bottom line. "How much to join?

**I was lonely enough to be
interested, but not lonely enough to
forget the bottom line.**

Here came the pitch. "Normally, $800. But for you, because we know you would be a great asset to our club, $700."

"That's very kind of you. But I can't afford that," I said.

"Well, after talking to you, I really think that it would be mutually beneficial if you could be part of our group of wonderful folks. So let me put you on hold while I speak to my supervisor."

While he was gone, I thought about how interesting a club like that might be, but how odd it seemed to have to pay anything to meet people.

"My boss says that he can come down to $600, but that's it. What do you think?" he asked.

"I think there is no way, but thanks for asking," I replied.

"Hang on, my boss is trying to tell me something," he interjected.

"You won't believe this. I don't believe it but he said that he will let you join for $400. That is unheard of. You can ask around." He was giving it his final and most enthusiastic pitch.

"Again, I thank you, but I really can't do it," I said.

"What could you pay?" he wanted to know. It must have been a slow night.

"Right now, about twenty bucks," I replied.

I think his boss must have told him it was time to wrap it up—this deal wasn't quite *that* mutually beneficial.

As I hung up, I told myself that I had plenty to keep me busy for awhile; that it probably wouldn't be that good an idea to have a busy social life right now anyway, even if it was an option.

Rationalizing was important at a time like that.

I was spending another weekend night alone on the sofa watching reruns on TV when I was startled by an unfamiliar noise. It turned out to be my phone ringing. I was so excited, I couldn't believe it. But I didn't want to come off as too eager, so I let it ring twice before answering.

"Good evening, ma'am." It was a disappointing opening line. The pleasant voice continued, "How are you this evening?"

Oh, brother, here it comes. Why do they always start out the same way?

"We are offering a special discount rate on our newspaper for a limited time only for folks living in your area," he went on. Was that supposed to make me feel special or something?

"No thank you," I said.

"This is a one time offer," he reminded me.

"I understand that, but, no thank you," I repeated.

He was relentless. "We have an installment plan. You pay only $2.95 a month."

I had run out of patience. I layed it on the line. "Look, I'm going through a divorce. I can't afford the newspaper, even if I had the time or desire to read it."

His attitude completely changed. "Oh, I'm sorry, so sorry to have bothered you," he apologized.

This blunt approach always worked. It was amazing. People reacted as if I had just told them I was dying of a terminal disease. Sometimes I felt like I was.

There was a time or two, on particularly cold nights, when I felt the need for someone to hold close. I was willing to snuggle with just about anyone who didn't have fleas or snail breath—two things I had to deal with when Taffy was the only warm-blooded creature around. Fortunately, I didn't go looking; nor did anyone come to my door when my standards were that low.

A friend told me I should get out more. I began to believe her when I opened my front door one morning to a large and very well built (man? no) cobweb. That afternoon I took a walk down by the harbor.

It was a lovely evening. I thought the beauty and the fresh air would make me feel better, but it didn't. I just felt lonely, with no one to walk with or talk to.

About a week later, I decided to try getting out again. This time, I drove down to Balboa Island. I had lived there once, and it had always been one of my favorite places.

It was fun at first, watching all the action: boats sailing on the bay, people relaxing in their front yards, kids speeding by on skateboards, a few die-hards still lying on the beach even though the sun was about to set. And the sunset was spectacular. But, the prettier it got, the worse I felt. I wanted to share the moment with someone—saying "ooh" and "ahh" all by myself was almost depressing.

Tears had started coming to my eyes when a couple walked by and stopped near me. I commented to them, "Isn't it a beautiful sunset?" which started a pleasant conversation that lasted through the dusk. I just needed a little "sharing fix," and even a chat with strangers lifted my spirits.

"A man who has friends must himself be friendly" (Prov. 18:24a).

Shaking All Over

With most of my nights free, I did a lot of reading. I bought every book I heard about that I thought might help me deal with my new lifestyle. And many of them were very helpful.

But one thing no book prepared me for was experiencing an earthquake all alone. When I was jolted out of bed at some horrendous hour of the morning, my body reacted as it always had in an emergency. I bolted up and ran to check on Paul.

But, he wasn't there. Fully awake by then, I realized he was at his dad's house. I stood under the doorjamb and prayed this would not be the big one. I didn't want to experience the big one alone.

I stood under the doorjamb and prayed this would not be the big one.

It is hard to describe how empty I felt, trembling inside and out, wondering how my child was doing. I believed he needed me, and I was sure I needed him. I had all that adrenaline running through my body and no one but myself to take care of. It just didn't feel right. (I was learning that there are many times in life when things just don't feel right.) When the shaking stopped, I realized I had a choice. I could stand there concentrating on my feelings of fear and anxiety and loneliness or go back to bed and wrap myself in the security of prayer. I chose the latter.

> *"Fear not, for I am with you; be not dismayed, for I am your God. I will strengthen you, yes, I will help you, I will uphold you with My righteous right hand" (Isa. 41:10).*

CHAPTER SIX

Dating . . . again?

"Hi, it's nice to meet you. I just had surgery; you wanna see my scars?"

Before the dust of the divorce had settled, before the concrete of the separation was even set up, before the ink was dry on the divorce papers, I had a great idea: "I need to get out there and date. Yeah, that's exactly what I need, a new man in my life!"

Was I right? No way. I have to admit that a wise woman suggested that I wait. But she was happily married. How could she really understand how lonely I felt? The one flicker of sound thinking I did have was on the subject of remarriage—I knew I wasn't ready to jump right into another permanent relationship. But from there my judgment basically went downhill for quite some time.

In many ways, finding myself suddenly single was like being a teenager all over again. My second go-round at the "awkward stage" was complicated by the fact that Paul was starting his first go-round, and so was Taffy!

Paul was almost always waiting for an important phone call at the same time I was. (I was glad that dogs don't talk—Taffy had some very outgoing friends.) My son and I argued about which of us spent the most time on the phone, and whose conversations were the least important. But, even when I won, he had a very successful technique for getting me off the phone: With Taffy's help, he would make so much noise playing, that I would be compelled to hang up. I tried covering the mouthpiece of the phone and asking him to keep quiet. That failing, I would resort to Mom's old standby, yelling. However, you only want to do so much of that when someone you don't know very well is waiting on the phone. First impressions are important.

All Kinds of Guys

I met men at church, at athletic events, at parties, at job interviews, blind dates (I tried that only once). And then I waited for phone calls.

When the phone didn't ring, I'd pick up the receiver to see if I got a dial tone. I figured if I could dial out, someone could dial in. Then again, one can't be too sure of these things. If I did get a dial tone, and the phone still did not ring, I'd use another phone to call myself—thank goodness for phone machines. The first time I borrowed my neighbor's phone to do this was fairly embarrassing. I couldn't remember my phone number. Fortunately, she could.

One afternoon, after I'd waited two whole days for an anticipated call, I took the big risk. I took Taffy for a ten-minute walk. Unbelievably, two calls came while I was gone, and one of them was from a guy. I was excited, but in a dilemma—what should I do? Obviously, I could return the call, but I'd always been told that a lady did not call a man except in an emergency. Of course, times have changed since that rule was made, but I didn't know it then.

In the end, though, my curiosity drove my fingers to dial the number. Unfortunately, the fellow just wanted to chat . . . about poetry, the weather, everything except asking me out for a date.

As I look back on this time, I realize what I really needed was a friend, not a love interest. But my sights were set on finding my knight in shining armor.

At first I was attracted to anyone who was attracted to me—good critique system, huh? And I met some real winners. There was a man who had no morals. There was a guy with whom I had absolutely nothing in common (with the possible exception that we were both human). There was a fellow I went out to dinner with as a result of dialing a wrong number . . . I've got to stop—this is too embarrassing.

One afternoon, after I'd waited two whole days for an anticipated call, I took the big risk.

I guess I figured that if these guys seemed nice, they must be nice. It didn't matter that I didn't feel comfortable with them.

One of the worst was the fellow I met at a party. He was gorgeous. He was also totally unreliable and unable to carry on an intelligent conversation, but who wanted to get picky? Did those things really matter? Not then. My lonely heart was willing to put up with him for quite awhile.

I waited from two hours to two days for calls promised at specified times. I got dressed up for a dinner date only to have him arrive so late I'd already gotten ready for bed. But I was too insecure to risk offending him. The best I could manage was to meekly mention that it would be nice if he would call when he said he would, and arrive when we'd planned.

During one of his calls, he said he had to get off the phone quickly and that he would call me right back. A few hours later, I decided this could very likely be considered an emergency, and one of those times when a lady could appropriately call a man. Still, I hesitated. Maybe he would think I liked him if I called. Did I? How was I to know? What an irrelevant question. I called.

He'd had to break off our earlier conversation because his washing machine was overflowing, he told me.

Was the problem now under control? I wanted to know.

It was, and now that it was so late, he was cancelling our dinner date. Not to worry, however; he would call me as soon as he returned from dinner with his sister.

Do you buy that? I did. Eventually, I "called" him on his inconsistency, and he never called me again.

Another fellow I went out with was not very handsome, but he seemed nice and polite, and he had a good sense of humor. Since we had met at a Christian function, I assumed we had similar belief systems. I was in for a rude awakening, which came when he asked if I'd be interested in doing some drugs with him.

I met a very conservative older gentleman at a political fund-raiser. (Not that I could raise any funds, but a friend thought it would be a good place for me to meet some nice guys.) He was nice, well-to-do, and respectful of my Christian beliefs, and we went out three or four times. He wasn't very exciting or interesting, but I thought perhaps that could be overlooked. Paul disagreed after joining us for dinner one night: my date divided his attention between a baseball game on TV and a business manual.

I met a few fourth-of-July guys as well—you know, the kind who come on like fireworks but fizzle fast. And then there were the guys who were just plain fast. I told one acquaintance that if he put a notch on his bedpost every time he slept with a gal, he'd be sleeping on sawdust.

At some point I started thinking. Something in my brain finally clicked. I began asking myself some questions: Why do you want these fellows to like you? What do they have to offer you? At last I began to break my habit of feeling that everyone had to like me and that I was supposed to please everyone I met. For a change, I began to consider what was best and what was right for me.

"For God has not given us a spirit of fear, but of power and of love and of a sound mind" (2 Tim. 1:7).

Another mistake I made when I started dating again was confusing vulnerability with honesty. I'd heard from a number of good sources that it's not a good idea to immediately reveal too much about ourselves to new friends. We should keep some secrets. But I was a pro at opening myself up right away to almost everyone, wrong people included. At first glance, it seemed okay to me. I mean, after all, there's a lot to be said for an open, vulnerable person.

Then again, the instant tell-all technique frightens some people away. I'd seen that first-hand when I shared my divorce story with people who were casual acquaintances.

What is the difference between vulnerability and honesty, anyway? I needed to know if I was going to temper my bare-bones openness without being evasive or deceptive. *The New College Dictionary* seemed like a good place to start.

Vulnerable 1. Susceptible to injury; unprotected from danger. 2. Insufficiently defended. 3. Liable to succumb to persuasion or temptation. (Well, there you have it. That's

111

why I was always in trouble.) *Honest* 1. Not lying, cheating, stealing, or taking unfair advantage; honorable; truthful; trustworthy. 2. Genuine; not characterized by deception or fraud.

Unless my dictionary left something out, I don't know who would want to be vulnerable. Honest, yes. No question there.

I have no regrets about my honesty in dating—with two guys in particular. I saved us some wasted, and possibly miserable time.

One was a blind date. He carried on a great conversation over the phone. He seemed interesting and quite funny, a borderline comedian. But when we went out for a get-acquainted tea, he was so quiet that I figured he must have had a roommate who wrote his lines for him. When he asked me out again, I told him I needed a break from dating for awhile. It was the truth.

I only got as far as a phone call with the other guy—the potential blind date. I brought up the fact that I was a Christian, and he commented that I must be very conservative. I agreed. He informed me that he was not. He said that he was basically interested in looking for a wife—was I looking for a husband? No way! The end.

❦

Another situation helped to open my eyes to my own desperation. I'd made a date to meet a girlfriend at a restaurant where a jazz band was playing, but she called to cancel just as I was leaving. I decided to go anyway.

By the time I got there all the seats were taken, so I stood near the door. I ordered a mineral water from the bar and settled in to enjoy the music. As the crowd grew, I found myself squashed between a well-dressed young man and an inebriated older man.

The young man wanted to talk world politics and the older man wanted to cry on my shoulder about the fight he'd had with his girlfriend. Being a nurturer from way back, I gravitated to the guy with the most troubles. My listening ear and sympathetic encouragement led to the inevitable. He started telling me how sweet and beautiful I was.

Being a nurturer from way back, I gravitated to the guy with the most troubles.

I caught myself blushing and thanking him for the compliments. How absurd! The guy could barely slur out his words, and I believed he actually meant what he said. He probably did not even *know* what he said. When I realized what was going on, I said good-bye and left. I couldn't believe I was so hungry for compliments that I would make conversation with someone who probably would have to be carried home.

"Therefore do not associate with one who flatters with his lips" (Prov. 20:19b).

One of the least intimidating and shortest relationships I had was with a man on the freeway. Actually, it started on a side street and ended on the freeway. Someone had made a crazy turn in front of him and I had seen it. I looked over, our eyes met, and we gave each other an "I can't believe it" look. Then we smiled. It just so happened that for the next fifteen minutes of driving, we kept coming up alongside of each other. And, of course, we smiled each time. If my memory serves me correctly, this is called flirting.

The experience was over almost as soon as it began, but since he was a very handsome man, driving a very nice car, my ego was built up a little by the experience. I was in a good mood as I exited the freeway. Then I started to analyze the situation. One side of me said, "Don't feel too confirmed; that kind of a compliment is quite superficial." Another side of me replied, "Hey, at this moment, superficial works for me."

I learned many things from my initial re-dating days. Dating again with others who are dating again is like going onto a battlefield. The major battle is over in most cases, but there is still an occasional shot fired from enemy camps (past relationships). And no matter where you touch a person, figuratively speaking, there is an open wound, a healing wound, or at least, a scar.

The injuries sustained in past relationships cause us to be fearful, because we don't want to experience any more pain. So, what do we do? We build walls, we hide in our "bunkers," we pretend to be someone other than who we really are, we wear shining armor. Or, we remain vulnerable. In my case, that was only because I'd failed to consult my dictionary before it was too late.

I had thought that my knight in armor was going to ride up beside me and carry me into the sunset. But, as one man after another rode right past me, I began frantically grabbing onto the tails of their horses and getting dragged through the mud. Ironically, I wasn't even checking to see if any of these men were actually knights.

I finally formulated a better plan. I decided to start with any new relationship in neutral. I would find out if the man I was dating had anything in common with me. Without unreasonably high hopes, I wouldn't be disappointed, and if things turned out to be terrific, I could always rise to the occasion.

I thought my knight in armor was going to ride up beside me and carry me into the sunset.

While I was dating-again, I heard some quotations that made a lot of sense:

"If someone seems too good to be true, he or she probably is."

"It doesn't matter how pretty the package is wrapped. It's what's inside that counts."

"Love isn't a feeling felt, it's an action learned."

When I stopped running around trying to fill my lonely void, I realized that God was willing to fill it for me. Once I understood this, it made sense to take some time to get to know my Lord better and to get to know myself better.

I wanted to become healthier—physically,

emotionally, and spiritually, and to be able to recognize good health in others. I still wanted the right man in my life, but now I could pray that God would send me someone in His timing.

All the projects that I had been putting off were looking better to me now: jobs around the house, books I wanted to read, and, particularly, extra time in prayer. Had I just taken a step in growth? Perhaps.

> *"Bless the* LORD, *O my soul; and all that is within me, bless His holy name! Bless the* LORD, *O my soul, and forget not all His benefits: Who forgives all your iniquities, who heals all your diseases, who redeems your life from destruction, who crowns you with lovingkindness and tender mercies, who satisfies your mouth with good things, so that your youth is renewed like the eagle's" (Ps. 103:1–5).*

COMES THE DAWN

After a while, you learn the subtle difference
  Between holding a hand and chaining a soul.
And you begin to learn that human love
  Doesn't always mean security.
And you begin to learn that kisses aren't
    contracts
  And presents aren't promises.
And you begin to accept your defeats,

117

With your head up and your eyes open,
With the grace of an adult, not the grief of a
    child.
    And you learn to build all your roads
On today, because tomorrow's ground
    Is too uncertain for plans, and futures have
A way of falling down in mid-flight.
    After a while, you learn that even sunshine
Burns if you get too much.
    So you plant your own garden, and decorate
    Your own soul, instead of waiting
    For someone to bring you flowers.
And you learn that you really can endure,
    That you really do have worth,
And that God really does love you—
    Just the way you are!

Author Unknown   Edited by Chris Stanfield

118

CHAPTER SEVEN

The House—
At Least I
Still Have
One—Falls Apart

I believe every man who leaves his wife should have to send her through a home-and-car maintenance course. To be fair, I guess a woman who leaves her husband should have to fund a home ec course.

About four months after my ex left, the roof on our house started leaking. Then my washing machine started rocking all over the garage. (Those things are not easy to move by oneself— at least not this self.) Next, my car started dripping oil.

Of course, there were also some less major problems, such as extremely hard-to-reach fluorescent lights going out, hoses breaking, and sprinklers malfunctioning. I discovered I was quite capable of handling many of these repair jobs, but others required professionals or kind neighbors. Like the problem with my front door.

For some reason, my door collected rain

water—inside. I was never sure why, but somehow, every time it rained, that door filled up like a rain barrel. And when it filled up, it would expand and the lock would no longer work. I could pull on that door with all my strength, but the hole and the lock just would not match up. There finally came a day when the door swelled up so much I couldn't get out of the house. I had to wait for hours until the sun dried out the door, and even then, I couldn't lock it that night. I called my helpful neighbor the next day. He had to take the whole lock apart in order to fix it.

Another day, I was getting ready for a very important job interview when the electricity went out. It didn't bother me too much until I went to pull my car out of the garage. That's when it dawned on me that garage door openers operate on electricity. I wasted quite a bit of time being frustrated as I tried to figure out what to do, before it occurred to me to call a garage door opener company. A very nice secretary gave me every detail I needed to free my car from the bondage of technology.

That wasn't the end of my garage door problems, though. One day as my son and I were getting out of the car into the garage, we heard a loud and dangerous noise. It sounded like something very heavy was ricocheting around inside the garage.

When I investigated, I saw that one of the

heavy-duty springs that open and close the door had broken. Half of the spring had scraped the back of my car, and the other half could have hit Paul in the head had he exited the car seconds sooner.

It sounded like something very heavy was ricocheting around inside the garage.

In order to use the garage door, I had to replace that spring—a tricky operation. And to top that off, not many months down the road, a spring on the other side broke. What are the odds of something like that happening twice? I was embarrassed to ask my neighbor for help after the front door incident, but some jobs just call for male assistance; he wrestled with the door while I wrestled with the spring. It wasn't long after that that I replaced the remaining two unbroken springs, this time with the able assistance of a terrific friend—male, I might add—whom I'd met at church.

Pests

When Taffy lived with me full-time, I had the house treated every three months for fleas. When she left for her six months at Paul's other house, I called the pest control service and told them they needed to come only one more time. While I was at it, I asked if they could also bring whatever they used to get rid of mice and rats. I had noticed telltale droppings in a drawer in my kitchen and bigger telltale signs in my garage.

I wasn't there when the pest control man came, so I did not know what kind of device he'd left for ridding me of the pests. But I was confident that whatever he'd left would do the trick. It didn't.

I was shocked one morning to see a little mouse scurry across my kitchen. I figured it must take awhile for the poison or whatever to work. After a week, thought, I called the service and explained my problem. A few days later I had some brand new bait boxes . . . but I soon wished I didn't.

I was greeted one morning by a baby mouse lying right in the middle of my kitchen floor. It was so cute, but it was dying. I didn't know what to do. In the past, I would have called upon my husband to take care of such a problem. As that was no longer an option, I thought about calling someone else but I couldn't think of anyone who would come to my aid so early in the morning. So I cried.

The mouse was just barely breathing. I apologized to it as I picked it up with a paper towel and put it in a plastic bag. I continued to cry as I tied a twisty around the top of the bag and gently put it in the trash. I was upset all day. When I called the service, they said that was not supposed to happen.

A month or so later, I noticed a bad smell in my garage. It got worse by the day, but I couldn't find the source. The stench finally got so bad, I asked my friend from church if he'd help me look. He was considerate enough to say that he'd go it alone if I'd cook him a meal. No problem!

It turned out to be the garage rat, who had obviously eaten the poison. He'd gotten only as far as a sleeping bag on a shelf before he died, and that had been awhile ago. I'm glad my friend found it instead of me.

Why did all of this have to happen when I was alone? Surely there couldn't be anything else, I thought, but then the phone rang. It was my neighbor, informing me of a termite invasion in our neighborhood. "I can't possibly have termites," I thought.

"Oh yes, you can. And you do," Mr. Termite Inspector told me. "Are termites worse than fleas?" I asked. "Oh yes, ma'am," he replied. He proceeded to tell me about the life cycle of termites, how they swarm, all about their mating practices, and what their droppings look like. I grimaced.

"Please. Don't make me feel bad because I want to kill these cute little prolific things that just happen to eat houses and garages for a living!"

Surely there couldn't be anything else, I thought, but then the phone rang.

I'd have to pay a small fortune to have the job done. On my limited budget, that was one of the last things I needed, but I figured that if finances got so bad that I had to sell my house, at least I'd have a whole one to sell.

Things That Go Thump in the Night

One night I was awakened by what sounded like a little bird trapped downstairs. I laid in bed thinking, "How in the world did a little bird get into the house, and why did it wait until this ridiculous hour to start peeping?"

As I lay there pondering those questions, the bird seemed to grow in size, judging by the sound of its peep. My imagination went to work, and I began to envision a gigantic monster bird. I finally got up the courage to get out of bed and sneak down the stairs to see what was taking up so much space in my living room.

You may have guessed that the peeping turned out to be my smoke alarm. Very annoying, but less annoying than a monster bird would have been. I nearly lost my hearing unhooking that thing. I guess the manufacturers know something about human nature that I didn't know: Unless the battery-is-dead noise is so loud as to actually drive people nuts and ruin their hearing, they will not go out and buy a new battery to replace the dead one.

On the subject of noises, I could not believe how the number of them increased when I was alone at night. Most nights I would crawl into bed exhausted, and as I lay there, with just enough energy to say my prayers, I'd hear my house's usual squeaks, thumps, tinks, etc. (I have a noisy house.) But on some nights, I'd hear sounds I'd never heard before. Sounds like someone rummaging around in the bushes outside my front door or climbing up the side of the house. Sounds like someone scratching on my window.

On those nights I'd be wide awake, trying to think of what I could do to defend myself when the culprit jumped into my room or scraped a hole through my window with his fingernails. I would give myself a pep talk: "Okay, Chris, you are a child of God, and you need to trust Him. It may not be your desire to get wasted right now in some gross manner, like you see on the nightly news, but if that is God's plan there is nothing you can do about it. (Well, now, that was reassuring.) I suggest you pray. Then recite some of your favorite scriptures." The pep talks usually worked. I'd fall asleep in spite of the noises . . . most of the time.

One night, after I'd said my prayers and quoted scriptures and stopped feeling fearful, I felt I had to investigate. The sound was so weird. It was as if someone was tapping on my window. I said to myself, "I'll just have a look. Maybe if I raise the blinds very rapidly, I'll scare whoever or whatever it is away."

"Maybe if I raise the blinds very rapidly, I'll scare whoever or whatever it is away."

I positioned myself close to the window, drew the blinds quickly, and stood very still.

My heart was pounding. When my eyes focused properly, I could see that it was a flock, troop, crew, herd (whatever the correct term is) of beetles. For some unknown reason, waves of them were flying headfirst into the window.

Maybe that's a beetle's version of "beating your head against the wall." Or, perhaps that's where the phrase "beetlemania" comes from. (Sorry, I couldn't resist.)

In any case, it was extremely annoying. But, again, far less annoying than a prowler would have been.

> *"Whenever I am afraid, I will trust in*
> *You. In God (I will praise His word), In God*
> *I have put my trust; I will not fear. What*
> *can flesh do to me?" (Ps. 56:3–4).*

Pruning

Tackling the yard work was hard for me. I'm not sure why, since I'd always done that job by myself, even when I was married. But somehow, on a lonely weekend, it was one of my least favorite projects.

One warm Saturday afternoon my friend David graciously volunteered to assist me, but when he started trimming my overgrown bushes and tree, I began to protest. I could not imagine my plants ever blooming again if he continued to trim at the rate he was going. After all, I'd trimmed most everything in the yard many times, and it looked okay to me.

He explained that when you prune really ruthlessly, you get rid of all the dead stuff and the plants grow back better than before. They would be healthier and have even more blossoms, he assured me. I was skeptical. My bushes looked like some of the haircuts I've had when I've asked for just a trim and she or he got carried away.

Later, I had to admit I was amazed to see the results. I spotted little buds coming from the bare branches in a very short period of time.

I got to thinking—I bet that's what's going on in my life. I was like one of my prolific bushes, growing all over the place with no real direction. Then the divorce came along, bringing some major pruning. The process hurt, but as a result there was potential for more fruit in my life, more blossoms.

Have you ever noticed that weeds are about the only plants that thrive without nourishment and care? Everything else needs food, water, sunlight, and nurturing. Likewise, resentment and anger are things we don't have to work at; those weeds just spring right up. But forgiveness and love take some time; they won't blossom without work.

"I am the true vine, and My Father is the vinedresser. Every branch in Me that does

130

not bear fruit He takes away; and every branch that bears fruit He prunes, that it may bear more fruit. . . . Abide in Me, and I in you. As the branch cannot bear fruit of itself, unless it abides in the vine, neither can you, unless you abide in Me. I am the vine, you are the branches. He who abides in Me, and I in him, bears much fruit; for without Me you can do nothing" (John 15:1–2, 4–5).

CHAPTER EIGHT

Recovering

Self-Esteem

During my divorce, and for some time afterward, my self-esteem was at an all time low. On a scale of 1 to 10, I'd say my score was about ½. I tried to be optimistic when I looked in the mirror, telling myself, "There's nothing here that a little hair-color, makeup, a new wardrobe, some weight training, and some image counseling couldn't take care of."

Most of the people around me seemed blind to how poorly I felt, though. They'd say things like, "I can't believe how well you're doing," but only because they didn't see me lying flat on my face on my living room floor, crying my eyes out, courting a rotten stomach, and reeling with a stress headache. How could they know? Most of the time I was playing the "basketcase in got-it-together clothing" role. It seemed a much safer approach than sharing what was really going on.

When I lived in Colorado, I could bolster my slumping self-image by walking past a construction site, which was always good for a few whistles and a hoot or two. The first few times I walked past a building site in California, nothing happened. (My guess is that California guys are spoiled.) But about the third time that I was near a construction site, I heard a whistle. I looked around, and there was no other woman in sight. I was too far away from the whistler for him to actually see what I looked like, but I wasn't about to concern myself with details. At that time, even a hint of approval was better than nothing.

Wait a minute. Didn't I hear somewhere that our self-esteem should not be based on what other people think?

> *"How precious also are Your thoughts to me, O God! How great is the sum of them!"* (Ps. 139:17).

Age

Age was a factor in my self-image as a newly single person. After all, I was over thirty. I felt a little better about this when I heard some wise statements on the aging process. An elderly man who was sitting next to me on an airplane said, "It's not how old you are, it's how you are old."

I also like what Laurie Anderson said, "I just turned 40. I can't decide if I feel more like 4 ten year olds or 10 four year olds." Helen Hayes had a good one, too: "Age is not important unless you're cheese." (I read these two quotations in an issue of *PARADE*, The Sunday Newspaper Magazine.)

What could I do about my age? Nothing. But there were certain things in the area of self-improvement that I could do. Knowing that my funds were limited, but that I still had health insurance, I thought, "First things first. Let's consider the really necessary repairs. I should get some allergy testing done. And my gums are feeling very sensitive lately—I should probably see my dentist. Besides that, my feet are killing me; I ought to check out the lurking possibility of bone spurs (my mom had them)."

Smile!

I started with my dentist. I'd always been told that I had pretty teeth, and I did not want to lose them.

"I can see why your gums are so sensitive," my dentist commented. "They're bleeding and you're losing bone. I'm going to have to send you to a periodontist."

The periodontist was nice, but very expensive. He asked about my current life situation and suggested that stress was probably playing a role in my problem. Great! That added even more pressure. How do you pull off not being stressed when you learn that your problem is largely due to stress?

"So, what can I do, besides get rid of stress?" I asked—doing away with the stress didn't seem to be an option.

"We'll have to scrape the teeth underneath the gum line," he told me. Well now, that sounded like fun and costly, too. "This procedure can be painful," the doctor continued. "We'll have to do it in two sessions."

"I'd prefer to do it all at once, if it's okay with you. I'd just as soon get it over with in one sitting."

"I don't recommend it, but it's your mouth," he replied.

I anticipated the worst; fortunately, the ordeal did not live up to my expectations. However, one bad thing did happen: as the doctor was scraping my teeth, he casually mentioned that he had inadvertently cut a piece of gum between two of my front teeth. He asked whether he should cut it off—after all, it was dead now and would eventually have to be taken off anyway. I nodded my head yes. What alternative did I have with a mouth full of dental devices and no knowledge of the consequences?

As my gums healed, I learned about the consequences—a large space between my teeth. It wasn't a huge space, but it was big enough that I was asked on occasion whether I had something stuck between my teeth. I would reply, "No, it's just a space, but thanks for asking."

Unfortunately, the doctor could not remember having cut off any gum.

"So, I suppose that means you would not consider taking care of the fee necessary to fix it?" I asked.

"You've got that right," he answered indignantly.

Oh, well . . . Is a space really going to affect my life that much? I don't know. We'll see.

Doing Time as a Guinea Pig

I had to muster up my courage before checking around for an allergy expert, but I finally managed it.

After filling out a myriad of forms, I waited in a cold little room, in a skimpy gown, for the standard forty-five minutes. For company, I had only *Humpty Dumpty Magazine* and *Medicine Today*—with the most stimulating article being "Know Your Adenoids." (I'd like to know what I'm doing here.)

A nurse came in to take my temperature and ask me questions, assuring me that the doctor would be in momentarily. (The problem is that doctors' offices have a different conception of the word *momentarily* than the rest of the world.)

... doctors' offices have a different conception of the word *momentarily* than the rest of the world.

Eventually, though, the doctor came in. She was large and soft-spoken, and she asked me the same questions that I answered on the forms and for the nurse. One of them sounded familiar: "Is there any stress in your life?"

"A tad," I replied.

"Well, that will make your allergic reactions worse," she informed me.

Of course. Just one of the many hidden effects of divorce.

She said I should start my testing the following week, which would involve being shot up with allergy-causing agents and noting my reactions. Once all my reactions were analyzed, I would then have to give myself shots with a serum, which, ironically, would be made up of the very things that I was allergic to. It sounded bizarre to me, but she was the expert. Her guess, from what I'd told her, was that my biggest problem was molds—not something you want to bring up in a dinner conversation.

The testing program was anything but fun. It took three or four hours each time and it was my job to note my reactions (unless the reaction was death—then the nurse would have to note it).

Some days I would have no bad reactions during the actual testing, but later my arms would swell up and itch where the shot had been administered. Other days, I would leave the office feeling absolutely miserable. I thought this was supposed to make me feel better! At least other people were going through the same thing.

One day when the heating system was broken and we testees were all huddled around a small space heater, I struck up a conversation with a gal sitting next to me. It turned out we had something other than allergies in common—we were both going through a divorce. Only hers was worse. My ordeals paled in comparison.

Her husband had left her for another woman while she was bedridden. Because she was unable to care for her children at the time, her husband got custody of them. Mary was in and out of hospitals, including psychiatric facilities, for a long time trying to discover what was wrong with her. Finally, a knowledgeable doctor suggested she go for allergy testing. It was a good suggestion. She was still having problems, but she was decidedly better.

Mary and I became friends. She gave me all the tips she knew about this testing stuff—she had been through it a lot longer than I had. And I gave her as many tips as I could about going through a divorce, since I was further along in that process than she was.

I eventually quit the program. For me, it hadn't worked. But at least I had given it a try, and I'd made a new friend in the process.

> *"Therefore we do not lose heart. Even though our outward man is perishing, yet the inward man is being renewed day by day. For our light affliction, which is but for a moment, is working for us a far more exceeding and eternal weight of glory"* (2 Cor. 4:16–17).

Getting My Feet on Terra Firma

Some months later, my feet were bothering me so much that I finally made an appointment with a podiatrist. "Don't tell me, it's stress. Right, doctor?" I asked.

"No, it's bone spurs. You should have surgery, unless your lifestyle does not require that you walk," the doctor said with a smile. Obviously a closet comedian. "I'd say now is a very good time to get this surgery over with, before you have a full-time job."

It sounded logical to me. "Okay, give me the details," I said, unenthusiastically. I figured that nothing could be worse than what I'd already been through. Oh, Yeah?

He filled me in on the details, downplaying the negative aspects as physicians tend to do when they have not actually experienced the procedure themselves. I informed him that I am unable to take pain medication. He informed me that, in that case, I could be guaranteed to experience pain.

I wanted to know how long I would be off my feet. The doctor, optimistically, told me it would not be more than about three weeks before I'd be back in regular shoes. In the meantime, I'd wear these special little sort-of shoes. I was beginning to get used to the idea of pain, and everything else sounded reasonable, so I decided to go for it.

I've made wiser decisions in my time. It was very painful, and the healing process took much longer than anticipated. Like so many things, I did not really appreciate how important my feet were until they were out of service. When I finally did get back into shoes, I had to wear tennis shoes for quite a while. I came to the conclusion that I had subjected myself to enough physical pain for awhile.

If I could have avoided going through all that physical pain while I was also trying to deal with the mental anguish of the divorce, I would have. Dealing with double pain was extremely difficult. But, I wasn't sure how long I'd have medical insurance, and I wanted to take advantage of it.

My self-esteem did not improve much because of the physical repairs, but it did improve as I got a better grasp on the fact that God loves me unconditionally. He had been there for me through each experience, and I felt more secure that He would always be there for me. I knew I could not have survived any of what I'd been through on my own strength.

"God is our refuge and strength, a very present help in trouble" (Ps. 46:1).

What's in a Color?

My hair started turning silver—oh, all right, gray—when I was eighteen. It didn't really bother me, because I got a lot of compliments on it. So, for many years, there was no question in my mind about what to do with my hair color. Leave it alone.

But, when I started getting turned down for modeling and acting jobs because of it, I started to wonder. Two things finally happened that greatly influenced my decision.

The first had to do with a movie being filmed in the Colorado town where I lived. The film company had brought along their principal actors, but they were using some locals for extras. One day the casting director asked if I'd like to have a small role. Well, if that isn't every actress-want-to-be's dream come true, I don't know what is.

Trying to appear calm, I asked what the part would be. She said that I would be an Indian. Wow! I just knew it would be a great part. I owned the local talent agency, and I had done some favors for this gal. I pictured myself riding a beautiful horse, racing like the wind through an open meadow. I'd be wearing a beautiful leather dress and a colorful headband, my hair would be flowing behind me . . . Whoa, boy! Let's stop right here. How could I play the young Indian with gray hair?

Ah . . . the light went on. She wanted me to be the *old* Indian woman, the one they have squatting near a campfire in nearly every movie with an Indian village scene. She has an old blanket wrapped around her head and body, with just the front of her shaggy gray hair showing, and there is a mangy dog barking at her as she stirs the venison stew. FORGET IT!

Scene two: agent-hunting in California. Everyone I spoke with said I should color my hair. I needed to have the all-American look, and gray hair was not part of it. On their advice, and against my better judgment, I decided to get rid of the gray.

If that gal was an expert, I'd hate to be the client of a novice.

I went to the beautician of a girlfriend who has beautiful hair, hoping I, too, would have beautiful hair afterward. I asked for blonde, like when I was younger.

It didn't come out blonde. It came out mud-puddle brown. I cried for quite a while.

The beautician did try to fix it, but the results weren't any better. I changed hairdressers and tried again. After a few attempts, the new hairdresser got a great color. But I had open wounds on my scalp from all the chemicals. He tried various products, but if he got the color, I got the wounds.

Then one day a gal in a restaurant asked where I had my hair done. I told her my hair-coloring stories, and she informed me that she just happened to own the salon next door to where we were having lunch, and furthermore, she was a hair-coloring expert.

If that gal was an expert, I'd hate to be the client of a novice. She turned my fading blonde hair to orange. When I told her that was not my best color, she proceeded to change it to midnight black!

I resorted to calling hair salons out of the phone book. Could anyone take the black away? I eventually found one who could, but he had to turn my hair to pure white to do it. It certainly was not the color of my choice, but it beat the alternative.

This fellow eventually came up with an acceptable color for my hair that kept my scalp intact. I stuck with him until he got married and moved away. Needless to say, I was sorry to see him go. Again, I bounced around from one hairdresser to another until I found another guy who knew what he was doing. I stuck with him until my financial situation slipped to a degree that I could either eat or color my hair, not both. I chose to eat.

With my checking account figures reading low, cosmetic changes and wardrobe changes were out. But I needed to make some changes to feel better about myself. What was left? My inner self. At least I could give that my undivided attention.

> "Do not let your beauty be that outward adorning of arranging the hair, of wearing gold, or of putting on fine apparel; but let it be the hidden person of the heart, with the incorruptible ornament of a gentle and quiet spirit, which is very precious in the sight of God" (1 Peter 3:3–4).

The Light's On—Is There Anybody Home?

Concentrating on my inner self was an enlightening experience. When I began this endeavor, I thought it was going to be less painful than the other things I'd been through. I didn't think that way for long.

I could not believe how many things I needed to work on. Even in a state of progress, I was still a recovering:

Perfectionist

Mega-nurturer (enabler or codependent if you prefer)

Talk-a-holic

Adult-child (in my case, a firstborn female from a divorced home)

Cookie monster

Worry-wart

Perfectionist and Mega-nurturer. For many years, I thought it was my responsibility to flit around my world like a sergeant-at-arms/fairy godmother combo. My plan was to make everything right and everyone okay in an orderly fashion. My, but it was a lot of work! And not always rewarding—the outcome of my marriage an obvious example. I was extremely glad to learn this was not my job. It was quite a load off my mind to realize that not everything was my responsibility, and not everything negative was my fault. Occasionally, I sneak back to "work," but I'm better at catching myself now.

Talk-a-holic. Usually I talk a lot because I have a lot of energy, I find almost everything interesting, and I like to share with others. But some of my verbalizing comes from a desire to keep the airwaves cluttered with noise, so that I won't be quiet long enough to hear what is really going on inside where the pain is. Once I found a support group where I felt completely safe to openly share my problems—everyone talked about their respective pain—I became less of a talker and more of an attentive listener.

*"Therefore, my beloved brethren, let
every man be swift to hear, slow to speak,
slow to wrath" (Jas. 1:19).*

Adult-child. I was very intrigued with this concept when I heard about it. In reading and talking with other people, it was obvious that many of us were raised in homes where we assumed adult roles while we were still children. Somewhere along the way, we missed the gradual maturing process. It certainly explained some things about me that I'd found puzzling: I wondered why I felt like a little kid in grown-up clothes. I wasn't sure I really knew how to play grown-up for real anyway. And yet here I was living and acting out a part for which I'd been given no script. Fortunately, the support group I joined helped me to better understand why I was the way I was and helped me to make desirable changes in how I related to myself and others.

Cookie monster. One of the tools for escape that I used for dealing with stress, sadness, loneliness, anger . . . was to make—and eat—cookies. I had my standards. I rarely just went out and purchased a bag of them; I wasn't about to stuff myself with just any old cookies. I'd make them as healthy as possible, but it had become a habit. When anything stressful came up, I'd move to the kitchen and make a batch of goodies.

It was suggested to me that, when I felt overwhelmed with the urge for treats, I should write out my feelings instead of eating. I came up with a better plan. Why not think about what to write while I was baking, and eat while I was writing?

As I became healthier, I started changing my self-talk: "Keep in mind that your body is the temple of the Holy Spirit. Do you think God would want His temple full of cookies? Probably not, since He wants what is best for you. You are worth taking better care of yourself." Gradually I learned to take a few minutes to focus on God and His provisions for me, rather than instantly running for the kitchen when I felt overwhelmed.

Do you think God would want His temple full of cookies?

"For you were bought at a price; therefore glorify God in your body and in your spirit, which are God's" (1 Cor. 6:20).

Worry-wart. A motto I had lived by was "Panic first, think later, if there is any time to think, which there usually isn't." For many years, I could have rewritten one of my favorite scriptures—Philippians 4:6–7. My version would have read: "Be anxious for almost everything. In the instances when you have your wits about you, pray, give thanks, and let your requests be known to God. But the peace of God, which could guard your heart and mind, will have a hard time because your focus is on the problem."

In retrospect, I can't believe my adrenaline maker didn't give out years ago. Fortunately, I was learning that not everything warrants a full output of energy and concern. Of course, this makes most sense when I focus on the fact that God is in control of everything—even people going through a divorce. I have a little saying that reminds me of this: "Don't Sweat the Small Stuff. Everything is Small Stuff. God is in Control."

For the reader who happens to be a psychologist and sees potential big bucks by having me as a client, don't call. I already have one. He is helping me to see which of my behavior patterns are based on fears from the past and which ones are constructive. My desire is to retain the child within me while not allowing my life to be controlled by childish behavior. I want to be the woman God would have me be.

"Being confident of this very thing, that He who has begun a good work in you will complete it until the day of Jesus Christ" *(Phil. 1:6).*

CHAPTER NINE

Looking for Work in All the Wrong Places

Even though I knew God accepted me, even though I knew externals weren't important, there was one event that often kept my self-esteem score hovering at the low end: an interview for a modeling or acting job.

I remember one interview in particular. I was auditioning for the role of a video spokeswoman, so I dressed in a business suit, got my makeup and hair just right, and off I went, feeling great.

As soon as I arrived in the parking lot, I knew it was a "cattle call"—a situation where the client has called a number of agents, who have sent out a number of actresses. In this case, hundreds.

I signed in and stood against the wall until a seat opened up. Once I had read the script a number of times, I started looking around. Everyone looked *so* good. I compared myself to every female in the room. Bad idea! Not one person had bags under their eyes like me. A gorgeous girl sitting next to me asked if I'd like to look at her modeling portfolio. I didn't want to, but "no" seemed like a rude reply. So, I looked. It didn't raise my self-confidence!

By the time it was my turn, my mascara was smudged, my hair was out of place, and my nerves were on edge. Technically speaking, I bombed.

The director was polite. He gave me the standard line: "Thank you. Someone will call you." Which usually means, "There's no chance, honey." But I read even more in his eyes. I felt he wanted to say, "Have you ever considered a career change? I understand that gardening is becoming very popular."

As I left the room my inaudible response was, "Not funny, and not even original. That's exactly what my high school guidance counselor said when she reviewed my Scholastic Aptitude Test scores."

I was mad at myself and depressed as I drove home, until I reminded myself that there would be other interviews and next time I'd try to avoid the comparison game. I recalled that the Bible has something to say about comparisons.

"For we dare not class ourselves or compare ourselves with those who commend

*themselves. But they, measuring themselves
by themselves, and comparing themselves
among themselves, are not wise" (2 Cor.
10:12).*

I was not earning enough money to pay all
the bills with my part-time modeling and acting jobs so I decided to pursue another career
interest—public relations. That was easier said
than done. I found that classified ads use the
term public relations pretty loosely; employers
are mostly just trying to glamorize a less-than-
glamorous position for which the title *salesperson* would have been more appropriate. I
followed up on a number of ads before giving up.

One number I called had a recorded message
telling me to leave my number so someone
could get back to me. A few days later, a man
called with a "golden opportunity." If I came up
with a mere $2,000, I could go to their training
school and learn how to be a convention spokes-
person, making up to $100,000 a year. I declined.

Another ad offered me a chance to sell flowers
to restaurant customers for $2.98 an hour. But
that wouldn't quite meet my budget requirements. An insurance salesman was looking for a
gal to make cold calls for him. Yet another man

wanted someone to assist him in selling water purification systems.

I finally switched to the education column. After all, I had a Colorado teaching credential and one year of teaching experience. That ought to account for something. It did—$4.95 an hour at a preschool.

Moving right along. I abandoned newspapers for awhile and began calling every business in my area where I might fit in as an employee. If they showed interest, I sent a resume.

Another ad offered me a chance to sell flowers to restaurant customers for $2.98 an hour.

This idea finally paid off. A fellow who had a small advertising agency offered me a one-time writing project while his regular writer was out of town. He said the job would pay $50 an hour and that it would probably take me about one hour. The only hitch was that he needed it the next morning. I took it.

The finished product was to be two different versions of ad copy for a technical device used mostly in the armed services. I'd never tried writing that kind of material and the information he provided was limited, but I gave it my

160

best shot—four-and-a-half hours' worth. When I finished, I called a friend who uses similar ads in his business. He thought mine were great. I felt good.

The next morning, I took the ads to the man and sat nervously awaiting his opinion. He liked them! I was elated.

I said, "It took me a lot longer than you thought it would, but I'll charge you for just three hours."

He said, "The whole job payed $50. What I said was it would *work out* to be $50 for *the* hour."

I don't know how I could have missed such an important point. Still, it was a good experience, and now I had a little more to pad my portfolio.

Diversion

One day as I was glancing through the newspaper looking for job opportunities, I came across the personal ads. The first one was so interesting, I read them all.

I was curious as to what men out there were looking for in a woman. If these ads were any indication, the answer is superwoman. An example: "Close Relationship Wanted by SWM 6' 1", 185 lbs. Looking for slim, intelligent, but real woman, 35-40 with no live-in children. Want someone to enjoy quiet times with, a feminine, positive, affectionate, and serious lady. You must be a down-to-earth, honest person who is strong on commitment and has a good sense of humor. Write with photo."

I was curious as to what men out there were looking for in a woman.

This ad created no problem for me. I didn't qualify. I went on to see what women are looking for. An example: "Wanted, guy who likes to play, dance, touch, interested in fireplace more than football, handsome in a rugged sort of way. If you are 35–48, 180–250 lbs., and are 5' 7"–6'3", I'm the girl for you. Call or write. Please, no weirdos or wimps."

Personally, I don't think there are guys out there who believe, or would admit, that they are wimps or weirdos. Can you picture a guy sitting on his sofa reading the above ad and saying to himself, "All right, she sounds great! I'm going to give her a call. Oh, no. 'No weirdos.' I can't believe it. Oh well, there is bound to be someone out there who likes weirdos."

Another ad that caught my eye was in the classified section: "WANTED-FAMILY VAN in exchange for antique Italian violin." Now, I'm not degrading these folks. They probably very much needed a van, enough to give up a family heirloom. But I have trouble picturing a man reading this ad and saying to his wife, "Oh, honey, listen to this—just what we've been waiting for. We can finally trade in the van for a violin."

Okay, enough fun—now back to work trying to get work.

I confided in a friend about my job-hunting woes, and she suggested I go to a businessman's networking meeting. I thought that was a great idea.

The meeting was exciting. The room was filled with friendly business people who had jobs that sounded interesting, but as I chatted with them, I realized that most of them worked in fields unrelated to mine. When I mentioned my background, they found it fascinating, but few of them had any idea who I could go to in my search for a position.

While the speaker gave his pep talk on creating energy and enthusiasm within the workplace, I let my mind drift a little. I thought about what fun it would be to answer the question "What do you do for a living?" with something unusual. Something like "I put straight pins, plastic collar holders, and paper in folded dress shirts," or "I neuter Mediterranean fruit flies." You know that there are people who have these types of jobs, but how often do you actually meet them?

So much for networking.

A friend of mine was kind enough to supply me with names of some public relations companies. I sent resumes to all of them, and finally, a few months later, I received a call from the owner of one of them. He knew my friend, and he invited me to come in for a talk.

The day of the interview, I put on my nicest business dress, painstakingly fixed my makeup and hair, and headed out with an optimistic attitude.

I waited anxiously for twenty minutes before my interviewer appeared. He apologized graciously for the delay and led me to his very spacious and well-decorated office. I was starting to pull all of my show-and-tell materials from my briefcase when we were interrupted by a phone call. "Please excuse me," he said. "I have to take this call. It's long-distance and I've been waiting for it all morning." I nodded my head and waited.

Eventually his call was completed, and we recommenced with the interview, only to be interrupted again, this time by his secretary. He excused himself and he left the office for a few minutes. I waited some more.

I finally managed to show him everything I thought he might be interested in, and he finally asked me all his questions. I waited breathlessly for the grand finale to this prolonged interview, and at last I got it. He pushed back his chair, smiled encouragingly, and said, "Well, from what you have said and shown me, I think you should continue to be an entrepreneur."

An entrepreneur! "So you don't see any possibility of me working for you?"

Now he was surprised. "Did you think this was a real interview?"

I wasn't familiar with fake interviews. This must be a trick question, I said to myself. But as I did not know the trick, I figured I'd best stick with the truth. "Actually, yes, I did."

He blushed just a little when he asked, "Jane didn't tell you?"

"I guess not. What was she supposed to tell me?" I was curious.

"I told her that I would see you, go over all your information, and give you any suggestions I might have. I'm not looking for any employees," he explained.

"Oh," I said "Well, thank you for your time. It

was nice to meet you. If you ever do have a position open that you feel I might be right for, please call."

I was not in a good mood as I drove home from this first non-interview. As a matter of fact, I was pretty well into a heavy pity-party. I started grumbling about what a waste of time, energy, and makeup it had been when I noticed a man standing next to the highway with a cardboard sign. When I passed him, I read it: WILL WORK FOR FOOD.

I was not in a good mood as I drove home from this first non-interview.

I apologized to the Lord for complaining. I started thanking Him for all that I did have, instead of grumping about what I didn't have. I was so blessed. It took the sign of a man much more worse off than I to get my eyes focused where they should have been—on trusting God to meet all my needs and praising Him for everything.

"In everything give thanks; for this is the will of God in Christ Jesus for you"
(1 Thess. 5:18).

166

CHAPTER TEN

Think on These Things

Pondering everything I have learned to date, I feel that there are a few very important priorities that I need to make sure are in order: God first, family second, friends third, and work fourth. If I spend the time I should in these areas, my stream of life will flow more peacefully.

I need to have faith in God. I need to trust that He is in control, even when circumstances would seem to indicate otherwise. As long as I have faith in Him, I will experience His peace, which passes all understanding, and the joy that comes from knowing that He is a loving, caring God who is in charge of the whole program.

I can either learn and grow from my experiences, or sit and stagnate. I'm choosing to learn and grow. You've heard that you can't teach an old dog new tricks? Hogwash. Whoever said that was an old dog who was too lazy to put out the effort to learn new tricks. It's a lot easier to play dead than it is to learn how to jump, roll over, speak, fetch, and leap through fiery hoops.

Learning and growing in life is not easy; often it's downright tough. But I can do it if I realize that I need God's help and the help of others, and if I remember that it takes a lifetime to fully mature.

I also need to remember that on my journey toward maturity, some of my steps will be big ones, but most of them will be baby steps. Sometimes I will need to rest, and sometimes I will even fall, and that's okay, as long as I get back up and keep heading down the right path.

"To everything there is a season, a time for every purpose under heaven" (Eccl. 3:1).

Reaching Out to Others

As my wounded heart began to heal, I so much appreciated the care and concern of others that I decided I should spend some time helping people myself. One of the first places I volunteered was at a nursing home for elderly folks.

I asked the fellow in charge what was needed most. He said visitors—people willing to go around and talk with the patients. That sounded easy enough, but it turned out to be very difficult.

Each time I went the emotions I felt ran the gauntlet from despair to joy. It was like being on an emotional roller coaster. One man constantly groaned and moaned from his bed. A lady in a wheelchair just outside of his room yelled through the open door, "I don't like that song. I wish you'd sing something else." Another lady told me to go away when I peeked my head into her room. A woman in the hall assured me that the grumpy lady said that to everyone.

I saw so many people who looked sad and helpless and lonely, that it was all I could do to keep from crying. Sometimes I had to go to the restroom to shed a few tears before going back out to visit.

But there were heartwarming times too. One time as I was walking down the hall, taking deep breaths and telling myself I could do it, a lady grabbed my hand as I walked by. "You are so pretty," she said.

My mouth dropped open. I could feel my cheeks turning red. How could she say that? I certainly didn't feel pretty at that time in my life.

I stopped and talked with her for a few minutes, and then, still clutching my hand, she said, "Thank you so much for talking to me."

If people could melt, I would have been a puddle. "You are very welcome. I'll see you next time," I said. And back to the bathroom I went, overwhelmed that someone could be that appreciative of a simple, short conversation. A thing so easy to give, and yet received as if it were a precious jewel!

I talked with very sharp, very fascinating people, and also with people who rambled on, making no sense when they spoke. But, as nurses would tell me, they all had an equal need for someone to sit and listen to them.

A group of ladies showed me their knitting, and some talked about the family they had who never came to visit. I felt sympathy stabs in my heart when I heard such stories. Some of these folks were cheery anyway, making the most of their situation.

One gentleman, Karl, had family, but they did not visit him much. He had a keen mind, with interests ranging from history to gardening: if he wasn't pointing to the old pictures on his walls and telling me stories about them, he might take me outside to a little backyard and show me the cactus plants. He told some great stories, and also gave me new insight into the world of the cactus.

He read a lot, regularly checking books out of the library. He wrote stories on a tiny desk he'd managed to squeeze into his small, shared room. He was such an alert and interesting man, and we so enjoyed our conversations, I could never understand why his family failed to visit him.

Still, each time I left the home I was drained. As I was driving home, I'd think it was the last time, that I couldn't take the pain again. But then I'd recall the smiling faces, or the faces that couldn't smile but could show with their eyes how much they appreciated a friend, and back I'd go again.

On one of my visits, a woman who couldn't speak pointed to a letter she had received. With gestures she indicated that she wanted me to open it and read it. I did. It was a beautiful letter from a childhood girlfriend she had not seen in thirty years. I cried when I read it and so did she.

Another lady, Mabel, was such a sweetheart. The first time I walked into her room, I was greeted with an incredibly big smile. She said, "You get more beautiful every time I see you."

I politely thanked her. Then she asked, "Isn't this the first time you've been here?"

I had to admit it was. That fact didn't bother Mabel. With much enthusiasm, she said, "I love you!"

Some people just have a way with words, don't they?

Mabel was ninety-seven years old. I asked her

one day what she thought had enabled her to live such a long, reasonably healthy, happy life. Her answer? "I like to spread love to others." It sounds like the truth to me.

There were two women in wheelchairs who, every time they saw me, would grab my hand and hold it for just a little while, kiss it, talk for a minute, and then move on. One lady would stroke my hair whenever we spoke. Human touch was very important to them—physical touch and the touch of conversation. These are presents we can give that don't cost anything but time. They're well worth the price.

"Therefore comfort each other and edify one another, just as you also are doing"
(1 Thess. 5:11).

I also became a group facilitator for some of the recovery programs at our church. Facilitators were chosen from people who had already been through each particular program, and I'd been through most of them. Going through programs for the second and third time, I discovered there was always something new to learn. I was in a different period of growth each time, which kept the process fresh, and listening to other people's stories was enlightening. There were always folks who had survived, or were learning to survive, situations that made mine look easy. I tried to share from my experience things that might help others move through their recovery more easily or more quickly. I found out that to help, or even to try to help, is to learn.

One of my favorite places to help out was in the nursery. During one Sunday service a month I got to hold little babies. That, of course meant other duties as well: listening to them cry, cleaning up little (and not-so-little) messes originating from both ends, pulling the aggressive types off the more passive ones. But when they were playing nicely or sleeping in my arms, it made all the other stuff worthwhile.

After one year in the infant nursery, I asked to be graduated to the toddler division. I was there for about six months before I moved to the two-year-old group. That was a particularly fun age group. They talk more, and when they do, they say the funniest things.

One day when class was over, and there were only a few children remaining in the room, a little boy came up to me and politely asked me if I could see his mother coming. "I don't know what your mother looks like," I told him.

He matter-of-factly informed me, "She's the

one with the green hair." (I think his mom and I have experienced the same hairdresser.)

After this group, I eventually advanced to the three-year-olds, which is another fun and interesting group. Sometimes they behaved like miniature adults, sometimes they acted their age, and other times they acted like a combination of both. Like the time the main teacher initiated an impromptu little Christmas play. She had a girl play the part of Mary, a boy play the part of Joseph, and a doll represent the baby Jesus.

**He matter-of-factly informed me,
"She's the one with the green hair."**

She wanted all the kids to participate, so the other boys became shepherds and the other girls became angels. The angels were to "fly around" while the shepherds went on their long journey to where Jesus was. She told the boys to circle the room until she told them to stop.

One little guy, Jimmy, asked a number of times, "Are we there yet?" The teacher explained that it was a long way. Jimmy finally just sat down on the floor. The other boys followed his example.

"Come on, shepherds, you are almost to the baby Jesus," the teacher urged them. The boys got back up and moved toward the manger scene. All but Jimmy.

"*All* of the shepherds need to come over here now," said the teacher.

Jimmy said, "Not this little shepherd. This little shepherd is tired, and he is going to go back home."

I can understand how Jimmy felt. Sometimes I feel that way about real-life journeys. Some are too long and tiring, and I just want to go home and rest. But I keep on going anyway. I hope that one day I'll be able to say what the apostle Paul said:

> "*I have fought the good fight, I have finished the race, I have kept the faith*"
> (2 Tim. 4:7).

Process—On the Road Again

Most of the time, I feel like Pacific Coast Highway—at least one of my lanes is always torn up. The difference is, I do not display a sign warning "Caution: Construction Zone." Maybe I should.

Don't you just hate those big metal plates that the repair crews put over the holes in the road when they are not working on them? You drive over those plates, and you can feel your suspension being wrenched.

Most of us know, at least vaguely, what a car suspension is. But allow me to quote from *Funk and Wagnall's Dictionary:* "A system of flexible members, as springs in a vehicle, intended to insulate the chassis and body against road shocks transmitted by the wheels."

My car is five years old and, although I have no idea how much it costs to replace suspension(s), my guess, based on previous repair bills, is too much. So, I bounce along on those metal plates "oohing" and "ahhing"—trying not to say any bad words. The road-in-repair experience is especially annoying when you can't change lanes due to heavy traffic. Uh oh, I feel another analogy coming over me.

Sure enough. I see my faith and trust in God as my "suspension system" as I go over the bumps and thumps of life. God has given me a suspension system of truths, intended to protect my mind and body against the shocks that are bound to occur as I bounce along the road of life. Sometimes I can change lanes to make things easier, but other times I can't. Then I have a choice: I can grumble as I go, saying bad words and being fearful of what the stress is going to do to me; or I can trust God to see me through whatever comes my way.

Another pitfall I need to be careful to avoid is that of watching too far down the road. Like the time I spotted some debris in my lane, quite a way ahead. I concentrated so much on the debris that I did not observe the large pothole and a lump of dried cement right in front of me. In kerplunk, and over bump, I went.

Sometimes I pay so much attention to the possible snares in my future that I run smack dab into a snare in my present—one that could have been avoided, or at least prepared for, if I'd been paying attention to today instead of tomorrow.

> *"Therefore do not worry about tomorrow, for tomorrow will worry about its own things. Sufficient for the day is its own trouble" (Matt. 6:34).*

Doors

I have heard many times about the open-door, closed-door theory in relation to trying to discover God's will for my life: If a door is open, I should proceed; if closed, I should stop and try something else.

I tend to be overly aggressive when it comes to trying doors. When doors are closed that I believe should be open, I try a little lubricating oil

179

just in case the angel in charge of doors was busy elsewhere when my door was suppose to have opened.

If that doesn't work, I get serious and pull out a crowbar. With this approach, I've managed to get some doors open that were pretty tightly stuck. Have you ever noticed how God gives us the freedom to do stupid things as well as smart things?

I occasionally wonder how many times the Lord has allowed me to get into bad situations. Judging from my track record, quite a few. Oh, well—looking at all those tough times through optimistic eyes, I see the many lessons I might have missed otherwise.

I jumped about a foot off the floor, my heart racing.

Speaking of doors, I have a large sliding glass one between my kitchen and back yard. One day, while I was doing the dishes, totally absorbed in thought, an extremely loud something happened on that glass door. I jumped about a foot off the floor, my heart racing. I turned to see a bird, who had not noticed the glass, lying on the ground. It wasn't moving.

180

I quickly opened the door and went to its rescue. I petted it's head and spoke gently to it as I cried. I picked it up and looked closely to see if there was any obvious damage to the body. I couldn't see anything, and it did seem to be breathing, however slightly.

I got a little towel from the house and layed the bird on it. I put water in a bowl and prayed for it to live, but the prospects didn't look good. I tried to console myself with the knowledge that although God cares about everything, even birds, there will always be death.

The next morning, I put the dead bird in a little box and buried it. As I did, I thought about the times I've banged my head against doors, knocking myself out trying to get to what I wanted—what appeared right. But things are not always what they appear to be.

Here was *that* principle again—I needed to trust the Lord in all areas of my life. I needed to seek His direction by praying, reading the Bible, seeking advice from more mature Christians, and watching for open doors. Trying to do my own thing, without guidance, was a weakness I needed to overcome.

"And He said to me, " 'My grace is suffi-cient for you, for My strength is made per-

181

fect in weakness.'" Therefore most gladly I will rather boast in my infirmities, that the power of Christ may rest upon me" (2 Cor. 12:9).

Risking

For exercise, I swim in a community pool. During one summer I'd swim in the morning in order to beat the crowds. I was usually getting out of the pool just as the very young kids were starting their lessons.

One very cute, precocious little girl, Kimmy, stood out in the group. She seemed to be a leader already; all the other kids followed her example. So, on the chilly mornings, the teacher merely had to persuade Kimmy to get in the water— usually with some compliment about her swim- ming ability—and voila! the whole class would be in the pool.

One beautiful, warm morning, I noticed all of the class sitting on the side of the pool. I heard the teacher pleading with Kimmy to get in the water, but Kimmy emphatically refused. The teacher tried halfheartedly to talk some of the others into getting in, but no one would comply.

She tried Kimmy again. "Please, Kimmy, you know how good you blow bubbles, and when the others see, they will want to blow bubbles too."

Kimmy's reply was still no. The teacher was getting very frustrated, since half the class time was already gone, so she finally asked, "Kimmy, why won't you get in the water?"

"Because of the sharks!" Kimmy replied in no uncertain terms. It took the teacher the remainder of the class time to convince the group that there were no sharks in the pool.

When it comes to taking risks in my life, sometimes I'm afraid to plunge in because of "the sharks in the pool." A piece of wisdom that has helped me considerably in this area, comes from H. Norman Wright. He says, "When we believe that our worth is a gift from God, we are free to risk because our worth remains stable whether we achieve or not."*

By reading the Bible, I can get an idea of what God thinks of me. And as I risk, I can rest assured that God loves me unconditionally, whether I succeed or fail.

> "For I am persuaded that neither death nor life, nor angels nor principalities nor powers, nor things present nor things to come, nor height nor depth, nor any other created thing, shall be able to separate us

So You're Getting Married (Ventura, California: Regal Books, 1985), 47.

*from the love of God which is in Christ
Jesus our Lord" (Rom. 8:38–39).*

Humor

More important than almost any other lesson
is this one: I must remember to laugh! Life is full
of things that can make me chuckle or grin.
Even when I'm down, I try to find enough energy
to pull up the funny file from my brain's memory bank.

There was that time in Colorado when we
were building a house. A tractor was working in
the back yard, and I had informed it's operator
that there was a temporary phone line about two
feet under the dirt. I'd even pointed out where it
was.

Within half an hour, the tractor man came to
my back door and told me that he had accidentally broken the line. I tried the phone. It was
dead. I went outside to have a look. Yep. The line
was completely severed.

I went next door to borrow my neighbor's
phone to call the phone company. I explained
to the service operator in detail what had happened. She asked, "How did you reach me,
then?" I told her that I was using someone else's
phone.

"Tell me exactly what the problem is," she said. Again, I explained, "A tractor worker has accidentally *completely severed, cut through, broken* the phone line. Could you please send someone out here to repair that one or give us a new one."

She had one more question for me: "Now, does that mean you are having trouble with incoming or outgoing calls?"

I bit my tongue as I replied, "Both."

Then there was the time when I had a faulty handle on my water purifier unit. The water came out when it was supposedly turned off. The installer had shown me how to adjust the handle, so I tried that a number of times, but to no avail. Eventually, I gave up and called the office of the supplier. The secretary suggested a different way to adjust the handle, and I did what she said, but within a few days, the leak was back. I called a second time. I explained the situation to the secretary. She put me through to the repairman. I retold the story to him. He wanted to know if I had adjusted the handle properly. I told him that I had adjusted it every way possible.

He asked, "The water comes out when the handle is at the off position?"

It's so hard not to be sarcastic at a time like that. I would like to have replied, "No, the water comes out when I turn it on and it stops when I turn it off. I find that very irritating." But I simply answered, "Yes."

Reading tabloid papers in the checkout line at the market is often good for a chuckle too. One of the most outrageous headlines read: "Blind Husband Regains Sight, Dumps Ugly Wife." The lady in front of me had a harder time with that one than I did. She was genuinely mad. She said, "Yeah, and I'll just bet that wife put him through school, raised his kids, and cared for him for years before he dumped her. And look at the thanks she gets. What a jerk!"

Although television news shows definitely don't specialize in humor, they do occasionally broadcast stories that make me laugh even when I'm not in a laughing mood.

For several days in a row, there were reports from a town in the South Carolina swamplands about sightings of a Lizard Man. It gave an opportunity for folks to say all manner of weird things. One young couple said they were late getting home from their date because the Lizard Man had jumped out in front of their car a number of times.

Another man must have heard that story, because he explained to his wife that the reason *he* got home late and that the fender was missing from the front of his car was because the Lizard Man had jumped in front of *his* car and had proceeded to rip the fender off and eat it before letting him go. I wonder if his wife bought that one?

Not to let this story die a natural death, another person reported having seen the Lizard Man and Elvis (who else?) walking along the road at night, hand-in-hand. The news coverage finally ended with an interview by an unhappy-looking reporter—who wouldn't be unhappy out in the swamps, in the steaming heat, being bitten by mosquitos and looking for Lizard Man clues?—interviewing a fisherman. The reporter asked the fisherman what he thought about all of this. The fisherman replied, "I been fishing in these swamps for thirty years, and I hardly ever see a fish, let alone no man that looks like a lizard."

I want to face my problems, pray about them, do what I can to remedy them, and then give them over to God. At that point I need to get on with life, to focus on the positive not the negative. Being observant of all the amusing things that go on around me and within me can help me do that.

Laughter is good medicine. During my divorce, I am sure that I put in more hours crying than I did laughing. But, as my sorrow seemed to reach new depths, so my joy seemed to reach new heights.

Laughter is good medicine.

"A time to weep, and a time to laugh"
(Eccl. 3:4a).

"Finally, brethren, whatever things are true, whatever things are noble, whatever things are just, whatever things are pure, whatever things are lovely, whatever things are of good report, if there is any virtue and if there is anything praiseworthy—meditate on these things. The things which you learned and received and heard and saw in me, these do, and the God of peace will be with you" (Phil. 4:8–9).

This scripture helps me to remember all the things in my good news department. I am alive, I have a great son, I have a house, a car, health, relatives, friends . . .

I was even given the unexpected opportunity to look for work in a more relaxed manner. I was receiving some money from a class action lawsuit which came about because of an investment

188

made while I was married. The broker had ripped-off many people, and all of us were getting back some of our money.

While I wasn't looking, a great job came my way. I wanted to thank one of my favorite ministries for the encouraging words I'd heard on their radio program during my divorce. So I took them some cookies. The secretary was kind enough to show me around their facilities. While in their television studio, I met the show's director. He was interested in looking over my theatrical resume and some samples of my writings.

My next meeting was with the president and members of the staff. I was given the opportunity to write and act in skits that would be incorporated into some of the television shows. This was one of my dreams come true—working in a Christian environment with some terrific people.

Another item from my good news department: I was dating, on a regular basis, my friend David. He and Paul got along great together, and that was particularly important to me.

Reflecting on all that I've been through, I can't honestly downplay the injuries. There will be permanent scars. But I learned a lot and I have plenty to be thankful for.

When the pain in my life has been most intense, it has been easier for me to keep my eyes on what should be my priorities. When there has been less pain, I think I have tended to take things and people for granted. I don't want pain, but, more than that, I don't ever want to take for granted the things or people that God has blessed me with.

For you who have read this book, I pray:

"Now may the God of hope fill you with all joy and peace in believing, that you may abound in hope by the power of the Holy Spirit" (Rom. 15:13).